# GOD'S PEOPLE IN MISSION

## An Anabaptist Perspective

Editors:
Stanley W. Green
& Rafael Zaracho

God's People in Mission: An Anabaptist Perspective
Copyright © 2018
Mennonite World Conference

All Scripture quotations, unless otherwise indicated, are taken from the Holy Bible, New International Version®, NIV®. Copyright ©1973, 1978, 1984, 2011 by Biblica, Inc.™ Used by permission of Zondervan. All rights reserved worldwide (*www.zondervan.com*) The "NIV" and "New International Version" are trademarks registered in the United States Patent and Trademark Office by Biblica, Inc.™

**Photos**
*First photo*: During the closing ceremony of the women theologians gathering in Guatemala, Albania Molina (left) and Antonia del Cid from Honduras bless each other in prayer for their ongoing ministries. Photo by Linda Shelly.
*Second photo*: Jerrell Ross Richer holds a flashlight as Pastor Ramón Umenda shares God's word with Esteban Mashacori and Charles Yiyoguaje during a youth retreat at Ninawachi (Place of Fire) Bible Institute in Huaticocha, Ecuador. Photo by Ron Borman.
The rest of the photos are by Jardely Martínez.

Book and cover design by Jairo Andrés Rodríguez Londoño
First Printing, April 2018

ISBN 978-99967-0-568-7

Printed in Paraguay
AGR S.A
Austria 2832 c/ Cnel. Cabrera.
www.agr.com.py
Asunción – Paraguay

# Contents

# Acknowledgments

This book has been possible thanks to the grace of God that has guided the writers to share gracefully their time, experience, knowledge and wisdom for the benefit of God's kingdom and the communities of faith. The financial support of *United Service Foundation* has been crucial for the publication and translation of the book. In addition, we would like to recognize the work of our translators. Tim Lind translated Chapter 7 from French to English. Rut Correa translated Chapters 2, 4, 6 and 10 from Spanish to English and Benjamin Shurance revised the accuracy of these translations. Karla Braun and Kristina Toews have been crucial editing and revising the entire book.

We are offering this book as testimony of God's grace, love, promises and hope for us and the entire creation. Finally, this book is a sign of our commitment as communities of faith in the process of seeking and becoming God's community of grace, peace and hope for our society.

# Missional Statements

As the Mennonite World Conference Mission Commission, we have been working and developing our Missional Statements since Switzerland 2012. We reached an agreement about our Missional Statements in the Netherlands in 2014. We cite below the 10 Missional Statements that resulted of the work of the Mission Commission committee:

## God's People in Mission:
### An Anabaptist Perspective

#### A STATEMENT OF THE MWC MISSION COMMISSION

God is a missionary God. Jesus is a missionary Lord. The Holy Spirit is a missionary empowerer. The entire Bible is a missional book. The whole church is a missional people. Therefore, by the grace of God, as an Anabaptist faith community:

1. **ORIGINS.** We lead people to know God as Father, the Creator who initiated in Christ a loving, comprehensive plan to restore peace to the universe.

2. **MEANS and MODEL.** We announce Jesus, the Son of God, as both the means and the incarnate model by which God restores peace. It is through Jesus' life, teachings, death and resurrection that the door opens to reconciliation, redemption, new creation and eternal life. Incarnational witness and service is our model for mission.

3. **POWER.** We walk in the power of the Holy Spirit in word, deed and being. We live and proclaim the

kingdom of God, forgiving, teaching, healing, casting out evil spirits and embodying suffering love.

4. **MESSAGE.** We invite all people to acknowledge Jesus as Lord, turn from sin, receive baptism upon confession of faith and follow him in life as part of the worshipping, serving community of faith. This community is itself a sign to the world. We announce God's kingdom by serving others with humility and gratitude, caring for creation and seeking to live in the world without conforming to the powers of evil.

5. **SCOPE and TASK.** We go beyond our communities as witnesses, following Jesus' instructions to make disciples of all peoples. We form new communities of believers, transcending boundaries of nationality, culture, class, gender and language. Because we believe that God has created and blessed cultural variety, we expect new forms of the church to emerge as we go.

6. **RISK and SUFFERING.** We trust God in all areas of life, living as peacemakers who renounce violence, love our enemies, seek justice and focus especially on serving and reaching out to the weak, poor, vulnerable, voiceless and oppressed. Because Jesus Christ suffered for us, we also accept risk and suffering for his sake.

7. **TEXT.** We hold and share the Bible as our authority for faith, life and mission. The Holy Spirit within and among us is the primary interpreter of the Word.

8. **WORSHIP.** We gather regularly to worship, celebrate the Lord's Supper and hear and respond to the Word of

God in mutual accountability. Our worship is an integral part of equipping us to participate in God's mission.

9. **UNITY and RESPECT.** We promote the unity of all Christians as part of our witness, and we respect the people of other faith traditions as we share the hope that is within us.

10. **FULFILLMENT.** We eagerly await Christ's return and anticipate the final fulfillment of God's kingdom when people of every tribe, tongue and nation gather in worship around the throne of God and of the Lamb.

*21/03/ 2014, in session at Dopersduin, Schoorl, Netherlands.*

In what follows, we will present two comments from some of those who were part of the project since the beginning. The first one is Hermann Woelke (member of the Mission Commission on behalf of Global Mission Fellowship, GMF) from Uruguay who says:

"Being part of the Mission Commission (MC) committee of the Mennonite World Conference (MWC) in all these years has been an enriching experience. Repeatedly, we have struggled with the challenge to promote, to focus and to give direction to the mission work of the many agencies and organizations that are part of the MC and MWC. The Statement of the Mission Commission called 'God's People in Mission: An Anabaptist Perspective' became an important instrument in this process of finding and giving direction to the mission work. The 10 missional statements are inspired and based on the 'Shared Convictions' of the MWC. The Missional Statements gave us a new sense of mission prioritizing the understanding that Jesus himself is our model who through his incarnation and practice during his time on earth can help us to promote incarnational witness and service as our model for mission."

Woelke adds, "the next step is to motivate and challenge not only mission workers, but also all the community of MWC to think, to preach and to do our church work in missional terms. We believe strongly that all those who will read this book will get and transmit the motivation and challenge for mission as expressed in the Mission Statements and as explained in this book."

The second is John S. Fumana (member of the MC on behalf of Global Anabaptist Service Network, GASN) from DR Congo who affirms, "It has been a privilege to serve the Lord under the MWC Mission Commission. Guided by the Holy Spirit, we have been able to make a statement regarding the 'Shared Convictions' of what Anabaptists around the globe believe the Bible says about mission. The conversation and reflections started in Basel, Switzerland, in 2012 and were concluded in Dopersduin in 2014. In this entire path, we felt God's presence and inspiration leading us to adopt this missional statement."

"How amazing it was to see the power of the Holy Spirit bringing people of different national and cultural backgrounds together as one body, Christ's body, and share common views on God's mission. This experience has strengthened my faith and encouraged me in my service for the Lord. Participating in this project, I felt the fulfillment of what Paul says in Eph 4:11–13: 'So Christ himself gave the apostles, the prophets, the evangelists, the pastors and teachers, to equip his people for works of service, so that the body of Christ may be built up until we all reach unity in the faith and in the knowledge of the Son of God and become mature, attaining to the whole measure of the fullness of Christ,' and 1 Cor 12:4–5: 'There are different kinds of gifts, but the same Spirit distributes them. There are different kinds of service, but the same Lord.' The Spirit of the Lord led us to agree and believe in unity in diversity." Fumana adds, "As Anabaptists, we hold it true that God is a missionary God and the mandate of the church is mission. The church of the Lord Jesus is a missionary church. He has sent us to make disciples of all nations."

## MISSION COMMISSION MEMBERS 2012–2015

On behalf of *Global Mission Fellowship* (GMF): Agus Mayanto (Indonesia, chair of GMF), Hermann Woelke (Uruguay), Adolphe Komuesa Kalunga (DR Congo) and James Krabill (USA). On behalf of *Global Anabaptist Service Network* (GASN): Ron Byler (USA, chair of GASN), Erlinda Robelo (Honduras), and John Fumana (DR Congo). As continental reps: Edgardo Docuyanan (Philippines), Don McNiven (USA), Max Wiedmer (France), Benjamin Mubenga (DR Congo), and Ofelia García (México). Richard Showalter (USA, chair of MC) and Rafael Zaracho (Paraguay, secretary).

# Introduction

The vision for this book was birthed in the Mission Commission of the Mennonite World Conference (MWC). The Mission Commission's vision was given life through a core of defining theological or missiological convictions that were shared in common among the members of the group:

- God is a missionary God.

- The life, death, resurrection and ascension of Jesus is given meaning by the missionary purposes of God.

- The primary agency of Holy Spirit is to empower the church for missional engagement with the world.

- The entire Bible is a missional narrative.

- The whole church is a missionary community.

This core of shared theological/missiological convictions, informally shared among the members of the Mission Commission, led to an interest in developing a more comprehensive register of those convictions that undergird and influence our foundations and approaches in mission. On 24 March 2014 after several years of yearning for a comprehensive statement of shared mission convictions, the Mission Commission adopted a document entitled *Missional Statements* in Dopersduin, Schoorl, Netherlands. The *Missional Statements* is a compilation of ten missional convictions, which articulate what we believe together about mission in the global Anabaptist mission community (see the section "Missional Statements"). In the interest of fostering unity within the global Anabaptist family during recent decades several resources have been published for the *Global Anabaptist Mennonite Shelf of Literature* on a variety of themes. Among mission practitioners, there has been a growing interest in compiling a fuller, yet still accessible, piece that sheds further light on the meaning and implications of each of these shared Anabaptist convictions about mission.

This interest does, however, beg the question: Why a text focused on mission? And, why now? A variety of responses might be made to these questions. We will attempt to address the key considerations of why this book and why now, while also highlighting the timely opportunity that is before us.

Though in recent years Anabaptists have been identified in the common mind by such distinctive as peacemaking, voluntary choice, simple living and community and discipleship, we believe that a key defining characteristic of the early movement was its fervent embrace of mission. Even while we continue to accent discipleship, we have muted the passionate, even sacrificial, commitment to evangelism. For the last half-century, there had been, particularly in the North, a troubling relinquishment of the missionary calling of the church. In this context, we believe that a text that can help us think soberly about our essential identity as the missionary people of God is an urgent need. Perhaps the conversations the book stimulates will reanimate us to align ourselves with God's purposes for the reconciliation of all humanity and the restoration of the created order. As God and God's purposes become again the subject of our sentences, we will be revitalized by God's Spirit for the mission which brought Jesus to our world.

One of the distinguishing marks of the Radical Reformation was its profound commitment to mission. In his description of the movement, Kenneth Scott Latourette accents the missionary activism of the early Anabaptists.[1] During the Reformation, the main concern of most Protestants groups was that the populace of a given political realm confessed the religion of the ruler within a certain domain (*cuius regio, eius religio* – as the prince, so the religion). Whereas the Catholic church was renowned for extending the influence of the church either through religious orders (mainly Jesuits, Franciscan and Dominicans) or through papal bulls enforced by means of violence, outside of maverick splinter groups among them, the Anabaptists deemed mission as essential to ordinary discipleship and sought to advance the witness to the gospel through vulnerable, often sacrificial and peaceful means. Unlike many Protestant groups who believed that the great commission was directed primarily to the apostles, Anabaptists assumed/understood the great commission was an injunction and a promise intended for every individual believer. These convictions compelled early Anabaptists to preach the gospel even when their witness to Jesus meant that they would literally follow him in death. The martyrdom they observed in the early church was seen as indicative of the fate of those sought to be faithful witnesses of Jesus Christ.

In 2016 we, the co-editors, were part of a walking tour in the city of Augsburg, Germany, that brought us to the likely location of an early Anabaptist event. That conference convened from 20–24 August 1527. Unlike most conferences which derive their names from the hopes and aspirations of what might be achieved, or merely from their geographical

---

[1] Cited in Hans Kasdorf "Anabaptists and the Great Commission in the Reformation," *Direction,* April Vol. 4 No. 2 (1975), 303. Available at: http://www.directionjournal.org/4/2/anabaptists-and-great-commission-in.html. (Accessed: 10/7 2017).

location, this gathering got its name from the outcome of meeting. The missionary conference of Augsburg, which came to be called the "Martyrs' Synod," resulted in an intensification of severe persecution, first in Augsburg where the gathering was convened, and then in every place to which the delegates went. Sadly, only two or three of the sixty leaders who met in Augsburg for the Martyrs' Synod, lived to see the fifth year of the movement. Despite relentless persecution, the resolute and daring witness of these early Anabaptists led to an expansion of the movement to many European countries. This missionary fervour and the growth of Anabaptist communities, particularly in the sixteenth century, were the fruit of three important distinctive that characterized the movement:

- Firstly, the early Anabaptists understood themselves to be bound by an unquestioning, unreserved obedience to the Great Commission. This obedience was required of every individual believer, not just a special class of priestly or ordained specialists.

- Secondly, the movement shared an interpretation of discipleship that was comprehensive. This perception of discipleship included being transformed in character by the example of Christ: affecting one's speech, habits and practices. Importantly, they interpreted *Nachfolge* (or discipleship) to mean not only conforming the whole of life to the example of Jesus – it also meant inviting others to experience the joy and blessing of freedom in Christ. Their desire to share with others their witness to the salvation through Jesus made them willing to risk persecution, even martyrdom. For them, discipleship required no less.

- Thirdly, Anabaptists recovered the centrality of "evangelism," or the imperative to cross frontiers for the sake of bearing witness to Jesus, as an important dimension of Christian witness. Whereas most Protestants during the early Reformation period were ready to enforce the principle that those who lived within a particular territorial realm professed (or practiced) the religious form dictated by the ruler of that realm, Anabaptists understood that the real issue was whether an individual, no matter where they lived, was submitted to Christ or not. This belief was bolstered by the influence of a text that was widely embraced by the Anabaptist believers, namely Psa 24:1 "… the earth is the Lord's, and the fullness thereof …" They took this to mean that the geography of witness was everywhere, regardless of the official religious practice that prevailed in any place. Imbued with this faith they went to every place where there was opportunity to share their witness to Jesus Christ with the result that by the middle of the sixteenth century Anabaptist missionaries were preaching in every state of Germany, in Austria, Switzerland, Holland, France, Poland, Galicia, Hungary and Italy. Several even went as far as Denmark and Sweden in the north and Greece and Constantinople in the south. Furthermore, some early Swiss Anabaptists mused about going "to the red Indians [sic] across the sea."[2]

Anabaptist engagement with the world during the eighteenth and much of the nineteenth centuries was marked by a relative quiescence forcibly imposed by the brutal persecutions that were inflicted on these communities through much of the sixteenth century. In the later nineteenth century, influenced by the missionary enthusiasm in the wider Protestant world, Anabaptists in Europe and North America (to which many communities had migrated in pursuit of the freedom to practice their religion), re-embraced the world and unleashed a century of comparatively robust mission engagement around the globe. These initiatives gave rise to a global family of Anabaptists and made possible the existence of a "Mennonite *World* Conference." During the closing years of the twentieth century, many Anabaptist communities in the Global South began to be involved in missionary activities. These developments created a space of subjectivity within which we now can engage needed conversation as subjects together (rather than in subject-object relations) about the shape of our common mission moving forward.

Next year will be 15 years since the formation of the Global Mission Fellowship in Bulawayo, Zimbabwe, five years since the initiation of the Global Anabaptist Service Network (GASN) in Basel, Switzerland and almost ten years since the initiation of the Mission Commission of Mennonite World Conference (MWC) in Asuncion, Paraguay in August 2009. During the decades leading up to the formation of the Mission Commission, we witnessed, as noted, the growth of

---

[2] Quoted by Hans Kasdorf in "Anabaptists and the Great Commission in the Reformation," *Direction,* April Vol. 4 No. 2 (1975): 303–18. Available at: http://www.directionjournal.org/4/2/anabaptists-and-great-commission-in.htm. (Accessed: 10/7 2017).

mission consciousness and the development of a faithful mission praxis across the many parts of the global Anabaptist family.

In the conversations leading up to the birthing of these entities, there was a recognition that Western mission often found itself allied with the colonial project, leading to some unfortunate and even tragic outcomes. To be sure, many Anabaptist mission initiatives struggled against an imperialistic spirit in their mission engagement. Sadly, though, whether wittingly or unwittingly, members of our Anabaptist family, socialized within a Western milieu, also shared with the others shaped by that milieu a perception that saw people from the South as primitive, infantile and weak. Even when driven by benevolent impulses, this lens and the power dynamic which was installed via the colonial enterprise, distorted relationships. As the Global South increases its engagement in cross-cultural mission, we now have the opportunity, as a polycentric community in mission, to discern what more thoughtful, sensitive and appropriate approaches in mission might look like. We can learn from each other, and from the past, in the hope of not repeating the mistakes of a previous era. We hope this text can provide the framework for these necessary conversations. It is this space, and these conversations, that this book is intended to serve.

The vision for this book, *God's People in Mission: An Anabaptist Perspective,* built as it is on the framework of the ten mission convictions, was to gather the reflections of several authors representing different continents. The goal was to bring together diverse voices and experiences from within the varied contexts of our MWC global family. A further goal is to make the book available in several languages spoken by members of the MWC. A number of the manuscripts were written in some of these languages and were translated. In the interest of ensuring wide accessibility, we hope eventually to have the text available in the three official languages of the MWC (English, Spanish and French) and, perhaps, several others. While the primary audience for the book is the Mennonite World Conference global family, we believe the book's basic biblical-theological foundations and its contextual reflections can serve a wider audience. We hope it can serve diverse groups as a resource for study and reference for workshops, trainings, Sunday school classes and seminaries by creating and promoting spaces for dialogue, reflection and commitments.

Stanley W. Green (Mission Commission chair)
Rafael Zaracho (Mission Commission secretary)

# Chapter 1

# Creation and the purposes of God

## Nzash Lumeya

> ***ORIGINS***
> *We lead people to know God as Father,*
> *the Creator who initiated in Christ a loving,*
> *comprehensive plan to restore peace to the*
> *universe.*

### INTRODUCTION

A major problem facing the Mennonite Brethren Church among Mbala people in the Democratic Republic of Congo (DRC) is to understand the origin and functions of Mbala people in God's creation. They are convinced that the Creator has cursed them eternally. Consequently, their existence on earth is confined to serving white people as helpers, maids and slaves. Along with this servile status is the conviction that they are inferior to white men and women. This naturally raises the formidable question: why should such an able people be tyrannized by such a demeaning self-image, and succumb to its tragic implications? Strangely they attribute this to the inviolable judgment of God and feel that their condemnation is clearly recorded in the Bible. We herewith review their understanding of creation and the purposes of God.

A close reading of the Scriptures reveals that the creation is a divine masterpiece, servant and a gift. The Bible opens its pages with the presentation of God, the Creator: "In the beginning God created the heavens and the earth" (Gen 1:1). The verb translated by "created" in English describes the divine power to bring the universe out of non-being. God is the only one able to bring into existence the heavens and the earth out of non-substance (Isa 65:17, Jer 31:22). The creation constitutes an amazing and miraculous work of God. Out of love, freely, harmoniously, and wisely, the eternal, sovereign God created the heavens and the earth. The cosmos belongs to God. The Creator of the universe sustains all things by his powerful word (Ps 24; Heb 1:4). The two first chapters of the book of Genesis affirm that God created a perfect world and humanity. God, the Creator made the first human beings, Adam and Eve, in his image. Sadly, Adam and Eve broke their relationship with their maker. The disobedience of the first couple brought divine judgment and groaning over the world. God promised to deliver sinners through a descendant of Eve (Gen 3:15; Gal 4:4). In making the covenant with Noah, the Creator promised to stabilize the world. After the flood, God restored the earth and decided to not destroy the creation because of men and women (Gen 8:21–22). God blessed Noah and his sons (Gen 9).

What about his son Ham?

## 1. ORIGINS

The curse on Canaan in Gen 9:25 has been misread in Africa. It has been misinterpreted as applying generally to all black peoples and specifically to Mbala Kipuka of Democratic Republic of Congo (DRC). As a result, many of them have gone astray and prefer to practice their local beliefs rather than to accept the good news of the Lord of Christ

Jesus. The curse on Ham/Canaan and black in DRC is one of the reasons that make them turn their back on a westernized Christianity. They believe that they live under an eternal divine curse. Most feel that because God cursed Ham, one of the sons of Noah, and because they are allegedly the descendants of Ham, one of the sons of Noah (Gen 9), they come within the sphere of this particular curse. What is the biblical response to curse? How could God, the Creator and Father, remove the so called "Ham's curse" from the Mbala people and groaning villages? Let us examine the text in its biblical context.

Noah said, "Cursed be Canaan! The lowest of slaves will he be to his brothers" (Gen 9:25). It is pertinent to remark that the narrative attributes the pronouncement directly to Noah instead of God. This is not a decree. The fulfillment of Noah's words depends not on themselves intrinsically but on God. Even though God is not named we assume that Noah is relying on him (Gen 9:26–27) to form and empower this curse. Noah is assuming that God will make Canaan become "the most conspicuous and lowest of servants"[3] The basic meaning of Noah's curse consists in distorting the relationship (brotherhood) in which Canaan previously enjoyed equal status with the others.

Noah desires this brokenness to be expressed by Canaan serving his brothers. The disgrace, as Westermann points out, is that the son who has dishonored his father must live in servitude to his brothers.[4] Who are these brothers that will benefit from the services of the accursed one?

---

[3] Franz Delitzsch, *A New Commentary on Genesis* (Edinburgh: T & T. Clark, 1888), 294.

[4] Claus Westermann, *Genesis 1–11* (Minneapolis: Augsburg Publishing House, 1984), 492.

Cush, Mizraim and Put or Shem and Japheth or both (Gen 9:5–27, 10:6)? There are inconsistencies in the text as it stands: (1) Ham is not punished but Canaan is; (2) "brothers" as stated in vv. 26 and 27 refers to Shem and Japheth. These two were Ham's brothers and not Canaan's brothers. Historically, the subsequent subordination of the Canaanites to the Israelites is understood as the fulfillment of this judgment. John Skinner affirms, "the servitude of Canaan to Shem at least includes the subjugation of the Canaanites by Israel in the early days of the monarchy. Beyond this everything is uncertain."[5]

Why is Canaan being cursed for Ham's sin? Why should Canaan be cursed for a sin that not he, but his father, committed? This question has been and is being asked in the Democratic Republic of Congo. The exegetes Cassuto and Westermann refer to God's blessing on Noah's sons as a plausible reason for not cursing Ham. "God blessed Noah and his sons" (Gen 9:1)[6]. They argue that Ham could not be cursed because God had already blessed him. Noah could not replace this divine favour with a curse. However, one asks why the transfer of punishment to Canaan and not to other Hamites such as Cush or Mizraim or Put? The rest of the Scripture does not seem to echo this text. It is difficult to answer with support of biblical texts.

In contrast with his curse on Canaan, Noah pronounces blessings upon Shem and Japheth (Gen 9:26, 27). In both speeches, Canaan is mentioned as their servant. But does this mean that Shem and Japheth are Canaan's brothers? The

---

[5] John Skinner, *Genesis* (Edinburgh: T & T. Clark, 1930), 186.
[6] Westermann, *Genesis 1–11*, 492; Umbert Cassuto, A *Commentary on the Book of Genesis* (Jerusalem: The Magnes Press, 1964).

answer to this question is debatable. As we have seen in the previous discussion, some maintain that Canaan, in this narrative, is Noah's youngest son[7]. But others contest the filial relationship of Canaan and Noah on the basis of the political genealogy found in Genesis 10:6.[8] They connect Canaan with Ham, his father and rest the case here (Gen 9:22). What is the function of this story in the larger context of creation?

The story of Noah and Ham is included in the primeval prologue, which deals with the universal themes of God and the origins of creation, human family, sin, judgment and covenant. Its function and thrust is to focus attention on the mysterious eruptive presence of sin and judgment in Noah's family. The inclinations of this community are not immune from sins. One must learn the tragic fact that the human heart is still evil, whether before or after the flood. When Noah discovers that sin has insinuated itself into the circle of his own family, he punishes it (Gen 9:25). As Westermann notices, the story of Noah and his sons stands before the table of the nations in order to highlight the fact that "the whole humankind derives from those saved from the flood."[9]

In originating diverse tribes, languages and nations from Noah's sons, this story knits its disparate known world into one human family, community. "The sons of Noah who came out of the ark were Shem, Ham and Japheth" (Gen 9:18). The table of the nations identifies in general terms the ongoing of the human race: "The account of Shem, Ham and Japheth, Noah's sons, who themselves had sons after the flood" (Gen 10:1). In addition, at the end of each of the tripartite sections, there is reference to Noah's sons. "From

---

[7] Skinner, *Genesis*, 184-186.

[8] Martin Luther, *Luther's Commentary on Genesis* (Grand Rapids: Zondervan Publishing House, 1958), 70.

[9] Westermann, *Genesis 1 – 11*, 482.

these (the sons of Japheth) the maritime peoples spread out into their territories by their clans within their nations, each with its own language (Gen 10:5). "These are the sons of Ham, by their clans and languages, in their territories and nations" (Gen 10:20). "These are the sons of Shem, by their clans and languages, in their territories and nations" (Gen 10:31).

This emphasis on unity within diversity is stressed also at the end of the tenth chapter of Genesis: "From these [that is the clans of Noah's sons] the nation spread out over the earth after the flood" (Gen 10:32). It seems to us that the story of Noah's sons stands as a common denominator to the historic-political view of the ancient world. Noah's sons "appear clearly as these great persons, who were obviously sharply distinguished from one another in the ancient Palestinian region."[10]

At this point, it becomes necessary to bring into focus the issue of the curse on Ham's descendants. One particular Western theological position, which states that Ham was dark-colored, appears to find confirmation on the ground of comparative linguistic speculation but not in the clear Old Testament text. Delitzsch says that Ham was black. He writes:

> The view that the three sons of Noah represent three groups of nations distinguished by the color of the skin, as the Egyptians divide the nations into the copper-colored, yellow, black and light-colored ... obtains a support only in the name [Ham]. Ham is the ancestor of the nations of the southern zone, and his name

---

[10] Gerhard Von Rad, *Genesis* (Philadelphia: The Westminster Press, 1972), 137.

might thus designate the dark-colored, though, according to the usage of the language, [Ham] means hot and [Hum] black …[11]

This statement lacks biblical support. The narrative does not seem to express any particular interest in the skin or hair colour of Noah's sons. To affirm that Ham was black is to do violence not only to the Old Testament text but also to the etymology. It appears inadmissible, in Hebrew, to translate the name Ham by black as Delitzsch proposes. Unfortunately, Henry Alford follows Delitzsch's classification and interprets Canaan's curse in terms of skin colour. For Alford, the curse on Canaan is not only upon certain Hamitic peoples of the biblical era but upon African races and today's blacks. He writes:

The curse, as matter of world-history, has more or less followed all the Hamite races. The Canaanites were under Joshua, and under the Shemite race of Israel, partly destroyed partly reduced to the most abject state of slavery (Josh. IX.21 ff.; compare Judges I.28, 30, 33, 35); and their remnants were subjected to the same lot by Solomon. The Phoenicians, who belonged to Canaan, with the Carthaginians and Egyptians, were subdued by the Japhetic Persians, Macedonians, and Romans, and the rest of the Hamite races shared the same lot, and do so even now, as e.g. the negroes and other

---

[11] Delitzsch, *A New Commentary*, 302-303.

African races under the yoke of the hardest slavery.[12]

Alford puts emphasis upon Western military supremacy over Africa as the fulfillment of Noah's prophecy over Ham's descendants. The fact of predatory colonial power seems to be as a persuasive argument. However, it could not be used in the debate about the curse on Ham's descendants. As Roland De Vaux has shown, military power in Israel's ancient history shifted from one country to another. The Israelites dominated the Canaanites and Hamites (Gen 9:25, 10:6), but Israel has also been enslaved by the Hamites, Egyptians and Babylonians (Gen 10:10, Hab 1–3).[13] It seems difficult to use militaristic imperialism as an evidence of the fulfillment of Noah's pronouncement regarding his sons. Influenced by Western racist bias in the nineteenth century, Delitzsch and Alford argue that the Noahic curse has fallen upon all Hamitic people. But where are these people? And how are we to find them? Delitzsch points out that skin-colour, climatic temperature and socio-historical situations are the basic criteria for determining whether a social unit is Hamitic or not. He continues by stating that a community's geographical position should be classified according to the differences between Noah's sons. Concerning the descendants of Shem, Ham and Japheth, he says, "Certainly the geographical point of view has a determining influence within the three groups, but it is only the case in a general

---

[12] Henry Alford, *The Book of Genesis, and Part of the Book of Exodus* (Minneapolis: Klock and Klock Christian Publishers, 1862), 42.
[13] Roland De Vaux, *Histoire Ancienne d' Israel* (Paris: Gabalda, 1971), 85–112.

manner that Japheth comprises the northern, Ham the southern, and Shem the central countries…"[14]

For Delitzsch and Alford, a people group such as the Mbala would be immediately called Hamitic. But why this classification? These scholars would point out that the Mbala are black, live in a warm country and are located in the southern hemisphere. They were colonized by Belgians ("Japhethites"). But how accurate are these criteria? For example, the Canaanites or Babylonians are called Hamitic in the narrative (Gen 10:10) but are not located in the southern geographical position.

A great debate exists today about the word "Hamite." When this word is used in relation to Africa, scholars agree that no consensus exists. Many scholars are reluctant to apply the adjective "Hamitic" to the Mbala people. Paul Bohannan uses it to mean Africans who speak Semitic languages "but who are ostensibly not of the Caucasoid racial stereotype and also not of the Negroid racial stereotype"[15] To identify the Mbala with the curse uttered on Canaan appears more as a fruit of Victorian Western understanding of the text, not a biblical explication. This false teaching regarding blacks being cursed entered among the Mbala people by American Southern Presbyterian Congo Mission and Baptist Mission Society.

## 2. THE STORY OF NOAH AND HAM

We turn now to the narrative itself (Gen 9:20–27). The story of Noah and Ham is included in the primeval prologue, which deals with the Creator and the origin of the universe, the human family, the judgment and relationship with Noah.

---

[14] Delitzsch, *A New Commentary*, 303–304.
[15] Paul Bohannan, *Africa and Africans* (New York: The Natural History Press, 1964), 66.

While God is compassionate, the rest of the creation struggles. One must learn the tragic fact that the human heart is still evil, whether before or after the flood. How could the accursed Mbala be transformed? Faith in Jesus Christ moves and removes all sin of any descendant of Adam and Eve. On the cross, Jesus Christ became sin and was cursed on behalf of sinners. Because of his death and resurrection every broken man and women who repents finds peace in God (2 Cor 5:17–21; Gal 3:13–14). Mbala people who believe in Jesus become blessed children of God. Peace with God does not depend of genealogy. Repentance to Jesus restores the broken relationship between God and a given sinner from Mbala or non-Mbala people. The human race is one. The Mbala people share with all other ethnic groups of this world not only the commonality of their humanity but also the sameness of their infection with original sin (Gen 3; 6:12; Rom 3:23; 1 John 1:8–9). Faith in God mends and establishes peaceful relationship between God and people. By faith, "Noah became heir of righteousness . . ." (Heb 11:7b). Menno Simons asserts:

> Faith accepts this gospel through the Holy Ghost, and does not consider former righteousness, but hopes against hope (Rom 4:18), and the whole heart casts itself upon the grace, Word and promises of the Lord, since it knows that God is true, and that His promises cannot fail. In this the heart is renewed, converted, justified, becomes pious, peaceable, and joyous is born a child of God, approaches with full confidence the

> throne of grace, and so becomes a joint heir
> of Christ and a possessor of eternal life.[16]

Indeed, because of Christ's suffering and death on the cross, the Mbala as well as all peoples can escape from death to life and from curse to blessing. Christ has voluntarily sought to become an object of the divine curse for all Jews; he has removed forever the obstacle which separated Gentiles from faith. He has made possible for Mbala people to receive the Holy Spirit (Acts 1:5; Gal 3:14). Faith in God is the only way to enter into relationship with the Father of Jesus Christ. No human being can enter it on the basis of meritorious activity. It is a God's gift internalized in us by the Holy Spirit.

### CONCLUSION: MISSION AND MBALA CHRISTIANS

The divine call to be a witness of Christ locally and globally does not depend on the colour of skin, but on obedience to the Holy Spirit. The presence of God, the Holy Spirit, enables Mbala Christians to become the community of God that is reproducing new Christians through the teaching of the good news beyond their ethnic group. This means that the Mennonite Brethren Christians from the Mbala people have received from God the missionary mandate. The Holy Spirit gives them the privilege to proclaim the death and Lordship of Jesus Christ across spiritual, linguistic, cultural, social, geographical and ethnic barriers (Matt 28:16–20; Acts 1:8; Rev 7:9–10). The power of the Holy Spirit will reconcile cursed sinners with our blessed Saviour and with one another as members of the body of Christ in the world. This solidarity with other Christians is essential in world mission. Both redemptive mission structures – centripetal and centrifugal approaches could be used to reach out to local and global

---

[16] John C. Wenger, *The Complete Writings of Menno Simons c. 1496–1561* (Scottdale: Mennonite Publishing House, 1956), 115.

neighbours. Because of its natural wealth, Democratic Republic of the Congo shares its territory with non–Congolese. Local Christians need to witness to tell them the good news of Jesus. The same love will be used to venture across the globe to preach the gospel to the nations. An effort will be made to protect the rainforest as part of God's mission. Our loyalty to the Lord and hope for the renewal of the creation could be expressed in forming mission teams that protect the environment. Mennonite Brethren Churches in Congo could participate in planting trees in depraved local and global communities threatened by erosions. These inter-ethnic mission teams could become pointers to the coming peaceful kingdom of God (John 17; Rom 8:18–27; Rev 21).

## STUDY QUESTIONS

1. What is the purpose of God's creation?
2. Why have the Mbala people been identified with the curse on Canaan (Genesis 9:25)?
3. What is your personal understanding of Genesis 9:25?

# Chapter 2

# Incarnational mission

### Rafael Zaracho

**MEANS and MODEL**
*We announce Jesus, the Son of God, as both the means and the incarnate model by which God restores peace. It is through Jesus' life, teachings, death and resurrection that the door opens to reconciliation, redemption, new creation and eternal life. Incarnational witness and service is our model for mission.*

### INTRODUCTION

In a Hyatt Moore painting titled "Last Supper with the Twelve Tribes," Jesus appears accompanied by twelve people from different tribes of the world. A bookmark featuring the painting poses the question: "What language will [Jesus] use to talk to each of them?" The answer appears on the opposite side: "Their own."[17] The idea of a God who has made Godself present, tangible and real in our world is at the centre of our beliefs and practices as faith communities. The incarnation tells us about this process in which God has become flesh and has come to "speak to us" in our language, context and culture. The doctrine of the incarnation is one of the pillars of our theology and it is where we can see most clearly God's

---

[17] For the painting and the bookmark, see Hyatt Moore, *The Last Supper with Twelve Tribes*, 2000. Available at:
http://www.hyattmoore.com/thelastsupper/Bookmarks. (Accessed: 10/28/2017).

love, care and purpose for our lives, for the life of our communities of faith and for all of creation.

In this chapter, I would like to offer some essential ideas and missionary implications based on the doctrine of the incarnation. First, I will briefly describe what we understand by incarnation in terms of the Bible and theology. Then, I want to offer some missionary implications for our faith communities.

## 1. WHAT IS INCARNATION?

The incarnation speaks to us of a God who comes to seek and rescue us. First, the God who comes to meet us does so in such a way that it breaks into our world and melds the spiritual and material dimensions. Second, the incarnation speaks to us of a God that became flesh in Jesus. Third, the incarnation speaks to us of the continued presence of God through his Spirit and his people. As members of the faith communities, the incarnation encourages us and challenges us to see the entirety of our existence as a testimony of the loving care and reconciling work of God.

Now let's look at these three aspects of incarnation.

### 1.1 GOD WHO SEEKS US

The first aspect we see in the incarnation is that *God comes to meet us*. From the first chapters of the book of Genesis, we see that God's purpose is to have a relationship with human beings and all of creation. Likewise, from the very beginning, we see the presence of evil and its terrible consequences. This vision of a God who comes to our encounter and to our rescue is a precious reality that fills us with the hope of restoration.

From the first stories in the Bible, we see a God who comes near and makes his presence tangible in the midst of people's daily activities. God has mediated and "materialized" his presence through his voice in the garden of Eden, the burning bush, the pillar of cloud and fire in the desert, among others.[18] God's presence is real in particular contexts and in the daily activities of persons and societies. Thus, we see that God comes to meet people when they are working in the field, looking for places to stay, looking for work in other cities. We also see that God comes to meet us in difficult situations such as famine, hostility between family members, persecutions and migrations. God comes to meet us wherever we are and his presence brings us comfort, protection and hope.

From the earliest biblical accounts, we can see God actively dealing with what sin had broken and fragmented. In the Old Testament, God comes and creates spaces for encounters of reconciliation and restoration. God, who is beyond our dimensions of time, space and culture, has come to make himself present and tangible in and through our dimensions of time, space and culture.

God has come to meet us in many ways and through many persons in order to create a community that could embody and proclaim this message of reconciliation: God comes to our encounter and to our rescue. This community is called to be a space where its members can live in a healthy relationship with God, with others, with themselves and with all the creation. This ideal of life for God's people was expressed by the Hebrew concept of *shalom*.[19] The life of

---

[18] These and other events that we find in the Scriptures and in which it is possible to see, hear and feel the presence of God are called anthropomorphisms.

[19] For a development of the concept of *shalom* see Bernhard Ott, *God's Shalom Project: An Engaging Look At The Bible's Sweeping Store*, trans. Timothy J. Geddert (Intercourse, PA: Good Books, 2005). In addition,

peace or *shalom* is a life of restored relationships which began with the very creation. This desire for reconciliation and restoration became more possible and tangible because, as Isa 9:6 says, "For to us a child is born, to us a son is given, and the government will be on his shoulders. And he will be called Wonderful Counselor, Mighty God, Everlasting Father, Prince of Peace." This Prince of Peace is Jesus. In and through Jesus, we are given the opportunity to experience the presence of Emmanuel: God with us.

## *1.2. GOD WHO BECOMES FLESH*

The second aspect we see in the incarnation is that *God has become flesh in Jesus.* The incarnation tells us about God's initiative to make his presence more real, active and tangible in our world. God has spoken in many ways through time and cultures, but in Christ, God has revealed himself in his greatest expression. In Christ, God has revealed to us his purpose for all creation and for all humanity (Heb 1). In a clear echo of the creation story, John tells us that the "Word (Jesus) was with God and the Word was God" (John 1:1). This "Word became flesh and dwelt among us full of grace and truth" (John 1:14). In Jesus, God has become human, the most definitive proof of God's active presence of God in our world. Thus, the incarnation tells us of a God who comes to meet us in a way that breaks into our world and merges the spiritual and the material. We affirm that in Jesus God has become present, real and tangible in our dimensions of time, space and culture.

With the birth of the Prince of Peace, God's character and his will to reconcile and restore have become more

---

Robert J. Suderman, *"Encarnando Ahora Vistazos del Futuro: Fundamentos Bíblicos del Shalom,"* in 15 Congreso Anabautista/Menonita del Cono Sur (Chile 2013).

visible. Through Jesus, God offers us the possibility of restoring our relationships which have been distorted and fragmented by evil, violence and injustice. In and through Jesus, God offers us the way and the possibility of salvation, that is, to unite and reconcile the entire creation with its Creator. Therefore, the incarnation affirms that God's intention is that our lives be reconciled ("merged") with our Creator, with ourselves, with our neighbour and with the rest of creation. From the very beginning, we can see that God created us as incarnated beings (fusion of the spiritual and material: "spiritual bodies" or "embodied spirits") in order to have in order to have these four-fold harmonious relationships.[20] In and through the incarnation, we can see that God confirms the original fusion of human beings' material and spiritual dimensions. The results of this "fusion" or overlapping of dimensions is what God called from the beginning "very good" (Gen 1:31).

The incarnation testifies that life, death and resurrection of Jesus are the maximum expression of God's desire to form a people of peace. Jesus, the Prince of Peace, shows us clearly what God's *shalom* is like: how it should be understood, incarnated and shared. That is, an alternative, embodied community that proclaims that the Prince of *Shalom* has come and inaugurated his government of *shalom* (kingdom of God). In the New Testament, more than the Greek term for "peace" (*eirene*), the term "gospel" best captures the Old Testament idea of *shalom* and refers to the "good news of salvation in Jesus."[21] In this context, one could

---

[20] John D. Roth, *Teaching that transforms: Why Anabaptist-Mennonite education matters* (Scottdale: Herald Press, 2011), 77–79.
[21] For those interested in exploring and deepening this topic, see Fernando Enns and Annette Mosher, eds., *Just Peace: Ecumenical, Intercultural,*

speak of the "gospel of *shalom*." However, what is the *shalom* of God?

The "Prince of *Shalom*" inaugurated his ministry by proclaiming what God's *shalom* is. Jesus began his ministry with these words in Luke 4:18–19, "The Spirit of the Lord is on me, because he has anointed me to proclaim good news to the poor. He has sent me to proclaim freedom for the prisoners and recovery of sight for the blind, to set the oppressed free, to proclaim the year of the Lord's favor." It was with these words that Jesus began his ministry and they serve as a summary of his call and mission. This is the gospel of God proclaimed and made visible by Jesus and the first apostles. The incarnation affirms that this is the essential message of the gospel of God expressed in love, hope and freedom for us and for our societies. We can affirm that from the very creation, God has been coming to meet us and has been seeking to create a community of peace in which its members can experience, embody, and proclaim what is presented in Luke 4:18–19.

### 1.3. GOD'S CONTINUOUS PRESENCE

The third aspect we see in the incarnation is *God's continuous presence through his Spirit and through his people*. The life and ministry of Jesus is a clear testimony of how God has come to meet us in the midst of a particular context and has approached people in the midst of their daily activities. God had communicated in many ways, but this communication reached its maximum expression when he became human in Jesus (John 1:14).

At the end of his ministry, Jesus sent out his disciples "to incarnate" following his example (John 20:21). Both the

*and Interdisciplinary Perspectives* (Eugene, OR: Pickwick Publications, 2013).

missionary mandate and the sending of the disciples took place after the resurrection. The Gospel of John tells us that Jesus came to meet his disciples when they were fearful behind closed doors. Jesus stood *in their midst* and said "peace to you" (John 20:19). The presence of the risen Jesus assured them peace and the continuous presence of God in their midst (compare John 14:26–27). In addition, Jesus showed them his hands and side (John 20:20), clear signs of the cost and the way of incarnation. The word and presence of Jesus brought the disciples the peace, hope and energy to open the doors and the joy to get out. In this context, John presents the incarnational model of mission: "As the Father has sent me, so I send you" (John 20:21). Unlike the parallel texts (Matt 28, Mark16, and Luke 24) in John, the emphasis is on sending, "as the Father sent me." This sending has an incarnational focus to go out and live in the midst of the people. It is in this context of sending that Jesus reaffirms his continued presence in the midst of his disciples through the Holy Spirit.[22]

The Bible shows the active role of the Spirit of God from the very beginning of creation. In Gen 1:2, the word used contains the image of the Spirit of God "incubating"[23] the process of creation. This notion of incubating conveys the Holy Spirit's presence, care and active role of the Holy Spirit from the very beginning. We can affirm that the Holy Spirit is still active incubating today in the midst of our daily activities. Jesus promises us that the Holy Spirit will be with us as we carry out the mission to incarnate ourselves in the

---

[22] Mortimer Arias and Eunice Arias, *El último mandato: la Gran Comisión, relectura deste América Latina* (Bogotá, Colombia: Clara/Semilla, 2003), 150–59.

[23] I am not aware of other versions using this term, see *Biblia Peshitta en español* (Nashville, TN: B&H Publishing Group, 2007).

midst of society (John 14:16, 16:13, etc.). As we seek to embody reconciliation and restoration in our contexts, we need to ask that the Holy Spirit continue to actively incubate the work of God in our lives, in our faith communities and in society. This vision of the God who comes to meet us invites us to appreciate how God has mediated and continues to mediate his presence in light of the ultimate revelation of Jesus Christ and through the Holy Spirit's guidance.

Although Jesus is seated at the right hand of the Father (Rom 8:34), God invites us to be his collaborators or incarnational agents in and through Christ; we do this by fleshing out *our encounter* with God and inviting others to have such an encounter. These encounters tell us of the ongoing work of the Holy Spirit who is actively "incubating" in our faith communities and societies to restore our broken relationships with God, with our neighbour, with ourselves and with the rest of creation. In this way, the followers of Jesus are invited to continue to cultivate incarnation in our time and context. As communities of faith we cultivate incarnation when we create spaces where we can experience with anticipation, as a foretaste of the future, the grace, the mystery and the mercy of God. As members, we work to mediate and embody the presence of God in our contexts with the vision and future hope of a "new heaven and new earth" where there will be total restoration and reconciliation (Rev 21).

As communities of faith, we seek to incarnate ourselves as instruments of peace. We work to mediate the presence of God by recognizing and remembering the mystery and grace present both in the incarnation and in the continuous work of God. Therefore, we are aware that our faithful attempts to name, mediate and communicate these encounters are partial. This helps us to keep ourselves open to the Holy Spirit and to the search for communal discernment in light of Jesus' life, death and resurrection. In this sense, we must incarnate ourselves following Jesus' model and remember that ". . . God himself has become incarnate among people even before we arrive, preparing their hearts to listen to the Word of God, revealing the Word to them through the work of the Holy Spirit, and transforming them by means of the power of the cross."[24] So we are invited, through the guidance of the Holy Spirit, to seek creative ways of naming, experiencing and transmitting those encounters that we have had as individuals and communities of faith for our particular contexts.

Next we will mention some missionary implications of the incarnation for our communities of faith.

## 2. MISSIONARY IMPLICATIONS OF THE INCARNATION

We have affirmed that the incarnation speaks of a God who comes to meet us. Our God has approached humankind in many ways and through many people to create communities of reconciliation and peace. In Jesus we have the maximum expression of God's communication in which God has decided to become human and to live among us. God has inaugurated his government of peace and reconciliation through the life, death and resurrection of Jesus and God invites us to be part of that government. As members of these communities, we are aware that the Holy Spirit empowers, encourages and invites us to renew our commitment and deepen our encounter with God, with others, with ourselves and with all creation. Therefore, the basic message we are called to live and proclaim is that it is possible to live in restored relationships.

---

[24] Paul .G. Hiebert and Eloise.M. Hiebert, *Incarnational Ministry: Planting Churches in Band, Tribal, Peasant, and Urban Societies* (Grand Rapids, MI: Baker Books, 1995), 373.

Here are some missionary implications for our faith communities.

### 2.1. INCARNATION HELPS US PRIORITIZE OUR TASK

In the incarnation, we see and affirm the image of a God who comes to our encounter and to our rescue. The vision and mission of Jesus is a message of hope and the restoration from the consequences of violence, injustice and evil present both in our lives and in our societies. We can affirm and see from the earliest biblical accounts that this desire for reconciliation and restoration is God's intention. Through the incarnation of Jesus, God breaks into our dimension of time and culture and meets us in a more tangible way. This vision of God that breaks into our world in order to offer us reconciliation and restoration delineates *what and how* our mission should be as communities of faith.

Let's mention at least two implications.

First, the vision of a God who comes to meet us encourages us to go out and meet those in need. This vision encourages us to remember that the nature of our communities is to be "sent" (John 20:21). We are sent to incarnate and therefore our call is to be communities that seek out those who are broken, afflicted and oppressed. We need to acknowledge and lament that all too easily our faith communities have occupied ourselves and centred our attention on ministries "inside the walls" of the temple, emphasizing "coming" to the building instead of the community "going." This "go" accentuates openness toward and the prioritization of ministries for the needy. In this way, our communities of faith are called to be and to cultivate *incarnational spaces* for the wounded and for those who have broken relationships with God, with others or with themselves.

Second, the vision of a God who comes to our encounter encourages us to be communities of reconciliation that maintain the tension between reality and possibility. When we go and meet the broken, we will come to grips with the devastating effects of evil, injustice and violence in different degrees and levels. In this way, our communities of faith must be constituted in safe incarnational spaces that recognize the tension between reality and possibility, the tension between who we are and what we can become. We are called to become – in the words of Ernesto Sabato – "specialists in hopes and despair."[25] On the one hand, in these communities of faith the members are aware and recognize that the Prince of Peace was broken and abandoned for each of us and this gives us the strength to be honest about our own brokenness and abandonment. On the other hand, members of these communities know that through the *resurrection* of the Prince of Peace we have the possibility of finding meaning and hope for our damaged relationships with God, others and ourselves. Furthermore, through the life, death and resurrection of the Prince of Peace, we can experience and offer others a hope of restoration in the context of a community of faith.

Jesus comes through the Holy Spirit in the midst of our communities and societies and shows us "his hands and his side" as signs of victory and hope for our fragmentation and the alienation born of violence and injustice. In this sense, Peter tells us that Jesus "himself bore our sins in his body on the cross, so that we might die to sins and live for righteousness; by his wounds you have been healed" (1 Pet 2:24). Knowing that, we can announce that Jesus as the

---

[25] Ernesto Sábato, *Apologías y rechazos*, 3a ed. (Buenos Aires, Argentina: Seix Barral, 2007), 107.

"broken bread" is a symbol of hope for our fragmented communities and societies. This is precisely the message of hope that we celebrate when we remember the Lord's Supper. Jesus, the Bread of God, was broken into pieces for us so that we can live in restored relationships with God, others, ourselves and all creation. Following the pattern of incarnation, these communities of faith become incarnational places of proclaiming and extending the hope of restoration. In addition, these communities create space and opportunities to find meaning and purpose in life *in the midst* of broken and alienated relationships.

## 2.2. INCARNATION ENCOURAGES US TO CELEBRATE GRACE AND TO EXTEND IT TO ALL AREAS OF OUR LIVES

That the incarnate God comes to our encounter speaks to us of God's initiative and has the emphasis of grace. As members of faith communities, we have the opportunity to heal others and be healed by others. It is essential to understand that this opportunity and responsibility to serve others is by God's *grace*. We become part of these faith communities because God has come to meet us through the Holy Spirit and through the other members of the communities of faith. Thus, we can affirm that, thanks to the fact that the Spirit has been incubating, we have the possibility of being part of these communities.

Let's see some implications.

First, seeing our abilities as grace or a gift from God helps us to have a healthy perception of others' abilities. This helps us avoid unnecessary competition because we will see others' abilities as tools given by God to be used in the service of our neighbours (1 Cor 12). Second, understanding and keeping in mind that our call to service is by God's grace helps us to recognize, celebrate and value different callings.

In this way, we do not expect everyone to have the same ministerial calling, and this helps us to eradicate the classification between secular and religious which is so damaging. The incarnation clearly and compellingly confirms our human nature, from the beginning of creation, as incarnational beings in which our material and spiritual dimensions are merged. Thus, our professions and hobbies can be seen as potential incubation sites where we can embody and proclaim the *shalom* of God according to the abilities that we have received by God's grace. In other words, as members of faith communities, we do not reduce the influence of our encounters with and calling from God to service "within the temple," but we *extend* it to our workplaces, our neighbourhoods, our countries. Thus, as disciples of Jesus we are called and *sent* to incarnate in all areas of our lives, to proclaim the "gospel of *shalom*" and to *invite* others to be part of the government of God.

## 2.3. *Incarnation encourages and challenges us to be incarnational agents*

The incarnation outlines our vision and mission as communities of faith inviting us to be incarnational agents. The life, death and resurrection of Jesus offer a model for life and relationships in our communities. Jesus sends us to practice incarnation just as he was sent to live among us. The incarnation calls us to put ourselves in the gap in our societies; we become incarnational agents because we have been encountered by God. This encounter is characterized by the image of a loving God who comes to meet us and to bring us hope, restoration and reconciliation.

Let's look at some implications.

First, the incarnation encourages us to encounter and to walk together in *growing harmony* with God, with others, with ourselves and with all of creation. The incarnation challenges us as communities of followers of Jesus to continually mediate and incarnate the presence of God. Thus, our communities of faith can and should seek to be and cultivate *incarnational spaces* for finding reconciliation with our Creator, with our fellow neighbours and with the rest of creation.[26]

Second, the mission and identity of our faith communities resides in understanding that our call, as followers of Jesus, is to embody the purpose of God in our own lives, the life of our communities and the rest of creation.[27] The mission of God does not come down to the creation of a missions department or commission, but it has to do with empowering all members to be *incarnational agents* in their different jobs and services. As members of these communities, we will work in the light of Jesus' life and ministry so that our *different interactions* can become spaces where the Spirit continues to incubate the possibility of deepening our encounter with God, with our neighbor, with ourselves and with the creation. This process of *incarnating* or cultivating encounters with God under the guidance of the Holy Spirit is not for the benefit of the community itself, but as public testimony of God's desire for peace and reconciliation with all of humanity and all of creation. In this way the life, relationships and interactions of the community

---

[26] I remember the poem attributed to Teresa de Avila (1515–1582) entitled "Christ has no body" and where the main idea is that we are the feet, ears, eyes and hands of Jesus in this world. Available at:
https://www.journeywithjesus.net/poemsandprayers/692-teresa-of-avila-christ-has-no-body. (Accessed: 1/28/2018).

[27] Benjamin Shurance directed me to the inspiring interview with Peter Harris (A Rocha International) on how incarnation and creation care are related. Available at: https://soundcloud.com/user-945730680/peter-harris. (Accessed: 1/28/2018).

with those who are "inside" and "outside" are a powerful public testimony of God's love and intention to create incarnational spaces of reconciliation, healing and restoration.

## CONCLUSION

The incarnation speaks to us of a God who comes to our encounter and to our rescue. From the earliest accounts of the Bible, we see God's intention to restore what violence, deception and envy had destroyed. In Jesus, we see God's breaking into our world in its maximum expression, and, in and through him, the government of God has been inaugurated. This government is characterized by grace and mercy, and in it, the Spirit of God enables us to be collaborators with God. We ask and seek, as followers of Jesus, that the Holy Spirit continue to incubate and actively merge his presence and work into our lives, our faith communities and society. In this way, we ask the Holy Spirit to renew our commitment and deepen our encounter with God, with others, with ourselves and with all creation.

The greatest contribution that the church can give to society is to faithfulness to our incarnational calling and purpose. This is, to be a community where its members seek, work, proclaim and embody the possibility of living in restored relationships with God, with others, with oneself, and with all the creation under the guidance of the Holy Spirit and following the example of the Prince of *Shalom*. By living as incarnational communities, we will be proclaiming the *shalom* of God. In doing this, we will cultivate incarnational spaces of restoration and we will create opportunities to grow in the restoration of all our relationships. I want to finish with a prayer asking: [28]

*Lord, begin with us:*
*begin with us, giving us the good news to our*
*material, spiritual, emotional and relational poverty*
*begin with us, breaking our hardened hearts made sleepy by*
*our propensity for comfort, security, the status quo and*
*seeing you as Saviour but not Lord of our lives*
*begin with us, proclaiming freedom from our*
*legalism, hard-heartedness, activism, uncontrolled*
*consumerism and competition*
*begin with us, opening our blind eyes and letting us*
*see our blindness and insensitivity toward injustice,*
*oppression and suffering*
*begin with us, giving freedom to our oppressed hearts,*
*minds, spirits and emotions*
*Lord, begin with us, proclaiming your year of good*
*favor in words and deeds in the power of the Holy Spirit.*
*begin with us, that we might be ministers of your*
*gospel who recognize that being considered as instruments*
*is an expression of your grace,*
*for that reason, we give you, and only you, all the*
*glory.*
*Amen.*

---

[28] Inspired by Walter Brueggemann, *Awed to heaven, rooted in earth: prayers of Walter Brueggemann* (Minneapolis, MN: Fortress Press, 2003).

## STUDY QUESTIONS

1. If the nature of our communities is to be sent, mention some practical steps in which we as communities of faith can promote awareness, responsibility, cost and joy of going (being sent) to meet the people in need in our contexts.
2. What would be some challenges of being incarnational agents in our particular contexts (workplace, ecclesial, academic, etc.)?
3. Mention some activities inside and outside the walls of the temple where we can create and promote incarnational spaces of reconciliation, restoration and hope.

# Chapter 3

# The Holy Spirit and mission

Stanley W. Green

**POWER**

*We walk in the power of the Holy Spirit in word, deed and being. We live and proclaim the kingdom of God, forgiving, teaching, healing, casting out evil spirits and embodying suffering love.*

## INTRODUCTION: MISSION IS ALL ABOUT THE WORK OF THE HOLY SPIRIT

The Enlightenment, sometimes referred to as the Age of Reason (1685–815), was marked in the West by a widespread questioning of established authority. The era saw the advance of a range of ideas centred on reason as the primary source of authority and legitimacy. During this period, there was an explosion of philosophic and scientific activity challenging traditional doctrines and dogmas. Champions of the Enlightenment argued for a society based upon reason rather than faith and for a new dispensation based on natural law and science constructed around experiments and material observations. It was also a time of religious change (and anti-religious fervour), as some sought to recast faith along rational lines. Many in the movement argued that the universe seemed to determine its own course without God's intervention. A number of novel ideas about religion developed within the Enlightenment, including atheism and a deism which sought to believe simply in God the Creator without any reference to the Bible or any other miraculous source. Instead, deists relied solely on personal reason to guide their faith.

Though the role of the Holy Spirit in the church and its mission was downplayed and neglected at various other times in the Christian movement, during the Enlightenment the very conception of extra-human agency was dismissed and disparaged with unprecedented vigour. As a result, the Holy Spirit became the "missing dimension" in the life and witness of the majority church which appeared to have sequestered Trinitarian experience and conviction to the archives of history.[29] It is heartening, therefore, that we now live during a time when the church in its various manifestations confesses the centrality, and even the indispensability, of the Holy Spirit in the mission of God. The World Council of Churches Central Committee meeting on the island of Crete, Greece, unanimously approved a new mission statement. The statement accords a critical role to the Holy Spirit in God's mission, putting it thus: Life in the Holy Spirit is the essence of mission, the core of why we do what we do and how we live our lives.[30]

---

[29] There were, no doubt, several renewal movements in which contrarian conviction and confession were practiced. Marginalized groups like the Hussites, Waldensians, Pietists and strains of early Anabaptism all adopted a more welcoming posture to the Holy Spirit and his/her role in the life of the individual believer and the witnessing community. Cf. Donald Bloesch, *The Holy Spirit: Works & Gifts* (Downers Grove: InterVarsity Press, 2006).

[30] *Together towards Life: Mission and Evangelism in Changing Landscapes*, New WCC Affirmation on Mission and Evangelism, submitted by the Commission on World Mission and Evangelism (CWME), 5 September 2012.

Writing for the Catholic church tradition, Pope John Paul II released an encyclical on 7 December 1990 devoted to the subject of "the urgency of missionary activity" in which the following assertion is made: "At the climax of Jesus' messianic mission, the Holy Spirit becomes present in the Paschal Mystery in all of his divine subjectivity: as the one who is now to continue the salvific work rooted in the sacrifice of the cross."[31]

In 2010, The Lausanne Movement at its Cape Town congress (deemed the largest ecumenical gathering in the history of the church) produced a broad-ranging statement that addressed the challenges and convictions of that segment of the church at the beginning of the 21st century. The statement made this strong declaration: "There is no true or whole gospel, and no authentic biblical mission, without the Person, work and power of the Holy Spirit."[32]

Early Anabaptists in their writings and in practice embraced the importance of the Holy Spirit in the life and witness of the church. Erland Waltner and Walter Unger observe that "Mainstream Anabaptists as orthodox Trinitarians confessed both the personality and the deity of the Holy Spirit, avoiding both unitarianism and tritheism."[33] They reference Pilgram Marpeck who "like Menno Simons and Riedemann emphasized the importance of the Holy Spirit

---

[31] *Redemptoris Missio*: *On the Permanent Validity of the Church's Missionary Mandate,* No. 21, Rome, December 7, 1990.
[32] *The Cape Town Commitment: A Confession of Faith and a Call to Action,* 2011. The Lausanne Movement. Available at: https://www.lausanne.org/content/ctc/ctcommitment. (Accessed: 11/10/2017).
[33] Erland Waltner and Walter Unger, "Holy Spirit," *Global Anabaptist Mennonite Encyclopedia Online* (1989). Available at: http://gameo.org/index.php?title=Holy_Spirit&oldid=143600. (Accessed: 10/10/2017).

in the Christian life...(noting Marpeck's conviction that)... (T)he Holy Spirit in His relation to the believer effects regeneration, assures of salvation, guides into truth, activates the conscience, purifies the heart, comforts, produces love, and gives power and joy in service." Present-day Mennonites and Anabaptists continue to uphold these convictions about the role of the Holy Spirit. In a summary statement adopted by Mennonite General Assembly June 18–24, 1977, Estes Park, Colorado, the following affirmation was made: "Apart from sharing in the Spirit, no genuine participation in the blessings of the gospel and the life of the new order of God's kingdom is possible. Let us therefore encourage one another to "be filled with the Spirit" (Eph 5:18).[34] This statement by one of the partner churches in the global Anabaptist family echoes a sentiment that was expressed by J. B. Toews at the eighth Mennonite World Conference in Amsterdam (1967), gathered around the theme "The Witness of the Holy Spirit." Toews stated then that "correct theology, even Anabaptist theology, without experiential knowledge of Christ through the Holy Spirit leaves the Church impotent. The life of a dynamic church is in Christ through the Holy Spirit"[35]

At the close of his earthly ministry, Jesus commissions his disciples to teach, to baptize, to make disciples and to "be my witnesses" (Acts 1:8). They are invited to advance God's mission of healing and hope in the world. They will continue the work that Jesus had begun. These human agents will

---

[34] *The Holy Spirit in the Life of the Church (Mennonite Church, 1977).* Available at: http://www.anabaptistwiki.org/mediawiki/index.php?title= The Holy Spirit In the Life of the Church (Mennonite_Church,1977). (Accessed: 10/9/2017).

[35] J. B. Toews, *Witness of the Holy Spirit*, 59. Available at: http://www.gameo.org/index.php?title=Holy_Spirit. (Accessed: 10/9/2017).

feature in the story of the growth of Christian communities and generations of Christians in a distant future will hail them, and many who came after them, as exemplars of courage and obedience. There were Paul, Peter, Philip, Lydia, Stephen. And, in a less distant past, the stories of Western missionaries like William Carey, Hudson Taylor, Adoniram and Ann Judson, David Livingstone, Amy Carmichael, Lottie Moon, Gladys Aylward and Mary Slessor along with the more than 200,000 missionaries sent more recently from countries in the Global South, including Brazil, South Korea, and India, South Africa, the Philippines, Mexico, China, Colombia and Nigeria[36] are held up as icons of missionary devotion. Most branches of Mennonite, Brethren in Christ, Mennonite Brethren and related churches also have their lists of missionary heroes or heroines. Without discounting these human instruments, however, both the commissioning statements of Jesus and the subsequent account of the expansion of the Christian movement amply demonstrate that the growth and development of the church cannot be explained apart from the agency of the Holy Spirit. Human agents no doubt have impressive gifts, and in so many instances, an inspiring record of devotion, and, where there was any advance of God's purposes, it was not necessarily despite them. What is very clear, however, is the fact that God's mission was advanced by a power and an agency that was above and beyond their human capacities even when it was through their gifts, talents and experience. Of course, the

---

[36] *The Surprising Countries Most Missionaries Are Sent from and Go To*. Melissa Steffan, July 25, 2013. Available at:
http://www.christianitytoday.com/news/2013/july/missionaries-countries-sent-received-csgc-gordon-conwell.html. (Accessed: 10/11/2017).

Bible testifies that Jesus entrusts this work to human beings: to the apostles, to the church, to every individual believer. Nevertheless, as the Biblical witness also shows, "the Holy Spirit remains the transcendent and principal agent for the accomplishment of God's mission in and through the human actors and in the history of the world."[37] Agreeing with this appreciation of the Spirit's role in God's mission, Emil Brunner offers a vigorous repudiation of the frequent neglect of the work of the Holy Spirit in the church's witness:

> Behind the conception of tradition as it lives in the minds of many people today there lies, concealed for the most part rather than expressed, perhaps even unconscious rather than conscious, a concern for the idea (which the New Testament can only sanction) that it is not merely a question of the continuity of the word – the maintenance of the original doctrine – but also of the continuity of a life; that is, life flowing from the Holy Ghost. The fellowship of Jesus lives under the inspiration of the Holy Spirit; that is the secret of its life, of its communion and of its power. To use a blunt modern word, the Spirit supplies the "dynamism" of the Ecclesia. Word and Spirit are certainly very closely connected; and yet in these pneumatic energies there is something which eludes expression in words, something in relation to which all words are inadequate, if not in fact quite

[37] Encyclical Letter, *Dominum et Vivificantem* (May 18, 1986), 42: *AAS* 78 (1986), 857.

misleading. There exists even in the New Testament a certain tension between Word and Spirit. "The kingdom of God is not in word, but in power" (1 Cor 4:20). The apostle Paul freely admits that he won the Corinthians not through words of wisdom, but through demonstrations of the Spirit and of power (1 Cor 2:4).[38]

## 1. THE ROLE OF THE HOLY SPIRIT IN THE OLD TESTAMENT

We first encounter the work of God's Spirit (referred to as the *ru'ach* of God) in the Old Testament where we see the Spirit active in creation. We are told that the *ru'ach* moved over the waters at the beginning (Gen 1:2). The Spirit was regarded as the source of life and the breath of humankind (Gen 2:7). Following the role of the Spirit in the earliest creative acts of God, the Spirit functioned in a variety of ways in the Hebrew Bible (see Prov 8; Isa 61:1; Ezek 37; Joel 2; 2 Chr 7:1). The Spirit was present in works of liberation and justice, leading the people of God. The Spirit also inspired wisdom, empowered prophecy, stirred life from dry bones, prompted dreams, and brought renewal as the glory of the Lord in the temple. The Spirit-filled prophets of the Old Testament anticipated and foretold the coming Messiah. They announced that he would be Saviour of the world and that he would be led and empowered by God's Spirit. These prophets also heralded the coming age that would be marked by the outpouring of God's Spirit, bringing new life, fresh obedience and prophetic gifting to all people, young and old, men and women for the service of God.

---

[38] Emil Brunner, *The Misunderstanding of the Church.* (Philadelphia: Westminster Press, 1953), 47.

## 2. HOLY SPIRIT IN THE NEW TESTAMENT AND THE LIFE OF THE CHURCH

The same Spirit of God, who was present with the Hebrew people from creation, through exile and the return to their ancestral lands, is the One who descends on Mary (Luke 1:35) and makes the incarnation of Jesus of possible. The consistency of the Spirit's presence at key moments in the story of God's people confirms that the Spirit's participation in creation and in redemption is a pledge of his/her companionship of the church in its witness in the world. Moreover, the realization of the promise of a new heaven and a new earth presumes the mediation and agency of the Holy Spirit toward this end.

The record of the Christian movement substantiates the fact that the Holy Spirit is indeed the principal agent of the whole of the church's mission. Moreover, the biblical witness makes it abundantly clear that God's mission finds its wellspring in the role and function of the Holy Spirit. That the Spirit's action is preeminent in God's mission can be clearly seen in the role the Spirit plays in the ministry of Jesus. At the initiation of Jesus' ministry, the Spirit is present in a way that confirms God's sanction and blessing on the ministry of Jesus. God authenticates in advance the claims that Jesus will make of being God's Messiah. In John's account, the Spirit descends on Jesus of Nazareth at the moment of his baptism. According to John's account, the voice of the God makes a post-baptismal declaration: "This is my beloved Son with whom I am well pleased" (cf. Matt 3:16–17). According to John, it is also the Spirit who then leads Jesus into the desert to clarify the nature of the mission for which he was sent. Then, when Jesus begins his ministry at the conclusion of this test, he announces in a synagogue in Nazareth that the animating power for his mission is God's Spirit. Reading from Isa 61, he highlights these words: "The Spirit of the Lord is upon me for he has anointed me . . ." He then provides content regarding the nature of his mission (good news to the poor . . . freedom for the prisoners . . . recovery of sight for the blind . . . set[ting] the oppressed free . . . [and] proclaim[ing] the year of the Lord's Jubilee) (Luke 4:18–19). There was nothing particularly unusual about the fact that Jesus read this text. It was well-known and beloved among the Jews of Jesus' day, who hoped for God's kingdom. Jesus, however, then does a most unexpected and startling thing. While all the eyes of those in the synagogue were yet fixed on him, he made this astounding declaration: "This Scripture has come true today before your very eyes!" (Luke 4:21). Jesus made an audacious claim. In effect, he said, "I am the one appointed by the Holy Spirit to fulfill this prophecy of Isaiah. I am the long-expected Redeemer of Israel." The passage from Isaiah, which Jesus applied to himself, highlights several essential features of his mission. First of all, he was sent by God in the power of the Holy Spirit (Luke 4:18). Even though Jesus was the divine Son of God, he was empowered by the Holy Spirit for his ministry. Even though his birth was a miracle of the Spirit, at his baptism by John in the Jordan River, Jesus received the Spirit in a visible, dramatic and public sign that attested to all who witnessed the divine sending (Luke 3:21–22). Scripture seems to suggest that from that moment until his death on the cross Jesus was led by the Spirit (Luke 4:1).

When they describe the risen Christ's meeting with his apostles, all the Gospel writers conclude the report of the encounter with the "missionary mandate" that Jesus issues to his disciples. That each of the Gospel writers conclude the story of Jesus' incarnate life with a vignette recounting Jesus' commissioning of the disciples for the advancement of God's mission of reconciliation, restoration, healing and hope[39] is key to understanding the purpose of the church in God's economy. Among the Evangelists, it is John who makes abundantly clear what is implicit in each of the other evangelist's accounts: it is the Spirit of God who is the agent of God's mission, in and through the witness of the disciples. In Luke's rendition of the post-resurrection instruction of Jesus to the disciples, it is clear that without the Spirit's empowerment the mission of the disciples cannot begin. The disciples are directed to wait until they are equipped with power from above (Acts 1:8). Luke's account wants to make it unmistakably clear, it seems, that a response to the mandate which Jesus entrusts to the disciples is only possible in the power of God's Spirit. The sending and the Spirit are inextricably linked in the mission of God. Fulfillment of the charge is, thus, unattainable apart from the Spirit of God. By the same token, empowered by the Spirit of God, it is impossible to not bear witness as we shall see when we engage with the post-Pentecost career of the church.

The mission mandate given by Jesus and recorded variously by the different evangelists, as noted above, embodies two key distinctives that are shared in common between them. In each rendition, the mandate for continuing the mission that Jesus began includes a universal dimension. Jesus commissions the apostles to continue the mission for which he was sent instructing them to go to "all nations"; "into all the world and . . . to the whole creation," to "all nations"; "to the end of the earth."[40] The second component

---

[39] Cf. Matt 28:18–20; cf. Mark 16:15–18; Luke 24:46–49; John 20:21–23.
[40] Cf. Matt 28:19; Mark 16:15; Luke 24:47; Acts 1:8.

in Jesus' mandate is one of reassurance. Jesus encourages the disciples with the reassurance that they will not be alone in the task. He promises that they will receive the strength and the means necessary to carry out their mission. The promise is that they will not be cast merely upon their personal gifts, strength or limitations. Jesus' pledge is one of capacitation for the task. The performative power in their mission will be that of the Spirit. Jesus promises that, through the Holy Spirit, he himself will be present with them to empower and equip them for their task. Mark, the evangelist, makes an observation that bears out the reliability of Jesus' promise. As the disciples undertook the mission of bearing witness to Jesus the promise is realized: "And they went forth and preached everywhere, while the Lord worked with them" (Mark 16:20).

Jesus directly links the mission which he entrusts to his disciples with the mission which he himself has received from the Father: "As the Father has sent me, even so I send you" (John 20:21). Addressing the Father, Jesus says: "As you sent me into the world, so I have sent them into the world" (John 17:18). Jesus' sending of the disciples is integrally linked with the agency of the Holy Spirit at work in and through the disciples. The proper engagement of the disciples in God's mission consists in their willingness to collaborate, in a spirit of submission, with Jesus who is present to them through the Spirit. As they do, they are given the reassurance that that Christ will be with them: "Lo, I am with you always, to the close of the age" (Matt 28:20).

The earliest history of the church makes it indisputably clear that God's mission is not explained by the vagaries of human abilities but on the power of the Holy Spirit. After the life, death, resurrection and ascension of Jesus, the most powerfully defining experience for the early church is the experience of Pentecost. This formational event for the embryonic church completely transforms the disciples, liberating them from a sense of loss, grief and despair at the absence of Jesus and infusing them with a new energy, vision, boldness and courage for bearing witness to all that Jesus said and did. The coming of the Holy Spirit not only liberates the apostles from their reticence and timidity, they are also empowered to become fearless witnesses and prophets unfazed by palpable threats to their own security (Acts 1:8; 2:17–18.). The experience of Pentecost renders the apostles unafraid and eager to share their experience with Jesus and to proclaim the hope that now animates their witness. In light of the post-Pentecost transformation in the lives of the disciples, we can confidently say that the unfolding chronicle of the growth and development of the church described in Acts makes it unambiguously clear that, rather than being an account of human agency and achievement, the story that is told is about working of the Spirit.

In some of the early stories of the witness of the first believers, we see very clearly the role of the Holy Spirit in prompting, guiding and capacitating these disciples of Jesus for their tasks. Luke records that when the members of the Sanhedrin are incensed by Stephen's testimony and prepare to kill him by stoning, Stephen was "full of the Holy Spirit, (and he) looked up to heaven and saw the glory of God, and Jesus standing at the right hand of God. 'Look,' he said, 'I see heaven open and the Son of Man standing at the right hand of God' (Acts 6:3; 6:8; 6:10 and 7:55).

In the story of Philip and the Ethiopian Eunuch (Acts 8:26–40), Philip is instructed to go south to the road that goes down from Jerusalem to Gaza. There he encounters the Ethiopian eunuch and helps him to interpret the Hebrew Scriptures revealing the testimony to Jesus. Similarly, we are told that the conversion of Cornelius comes after a vision given to Simon Peter who is then directed to go to the home of Cornelius where God reveals to him that these Gentiles have already been chosen for incorporation into the body of Christ and are made members of God's family and household (Acts 10:10–16).

We see also the impetus and critical role of the Holy Spirit in the first, intentional engagement in global, cross-cultural mission which emerged from the multicultural community of followers of Jesus gathered in Antioch. According to Acts 13:2–3 the newly minted "Christians" were worshiping the Lord and fasting when the Holy Spirit said, "Set apart for me Barnabas and Saul for the work to which I have called them." So after they had fasted and prayed, they placed their hands on them and sent them off.

As a result of this new phase of cross-cultural mission introduced new questions were introduced, and even controversy entered into the life of the early church. Fairly quickly, queries arose about the basis on which Gentiles could be incorporated into the church. Disputations arose based on questions regarding whether non-Jewish believers needed to be circumcised and what ritual observances and stipulations of Jewish law they needed to observe and comply with. The resulting contention led to the first ecumenical council being convened in Jerusalem with apostolic leadership. At the first Council, which gathers the members of the different churches together with the apostles in Jerusalem, a decision was taken which is hailed as the fruit of consensus derived from the Spirit's guidance. In this most critical, course-determining decision by the fledgling church, a pivotal consensus verdict is reached. The result is attributed not to the eloquence or persuasive rhetoric of one or other of the human participants but notably to the role of the Spirit in that seminal gathering (Acts 15:28–29). It seems safe to surmise that the sequence named in the reporting of the determination that was reached is not coincidental. There appears to be intentionality in how the writer of Acts reports progression toward the resolution: *"It seemed good to the Holy Spirit and to us not to burden you with anything . . ."* (Acts 15:28). In its first fateful decision, the church chose to move toward what the Holy Spirit had already clarified. The Spirit's prompting preceded human wisdom and discernment.

## 3. THE HOLY SPIRIT AT WORK IN THE CHURCH *AND* IN THE WORLD

Before concluding, it is essential that one final important observation be made regarding the locus of the Spirit's work. The Spirit is present in a special way in the church bringing consolation, comfort and connection to Jesus, forming believers in the image of Christ and teaching the faithful in the pathways of God. It would be an egregious fault, however if the particular activity of the Spirit within the body of Christ was separated from the universal activity of the Spirit in the world. The Spirit's presence and activity is not limited solely to individuals or the community of the believers: he/she is also present and active in society among peoples, cultures and religions and within history. Or, as Vatican II put it, the risen Christ "is now at work in human hearts through the strength of his Spirit, not only instilling a desire for the world to come but also thereby animating, purifying and reinforcing the noble aspirations which drive the human family to make its life one that is more human and to direct the whole earth to this end."[41] Stephen Bevans asserts that the Spirit is at work in the church but is also very much

---

[41] Cf. Second Vatican Ecumenical Council, Dogmatic Constitution on the Church *Lumen Gentium*, 17; Decree on the Missionary Activity of the Church *Ad Gentes*, 3, 15.

involved in our world. The Holy Spirit creates and shapes the church according to the purposes of God; however, he/she is also at work as the "Spirit of mission" involved in all aspects of our universe. In speaking about the scope of the Holy Spirit's involvement, Bevans asserts that the Holy Spirit is concerned with all things and uses the term "transcending immanence" to describe the way the Spirit is engaged in the world today. By this, he means that "the Spirit of God is so involved in the world (immanence) that we need constantly to be amazed and challenged by God's presence (transcendence). He goes on to make the following affirmation: "The church's mission is world mission in the fullest sense; one might even speak of cosmic mission. Nation building, earth keeping, ecological action, education, preserving and transforming culture, enhancing the quality of life, cultivation of the arts – all these are fields of activity for those who are given to the Spirit."[42]

## CONCLUSION: ON NOT SHORTCHANGING OURSELVES AND GOD'S MISSION

I have always loved being around, and preferably in, water. When I became aware of the alluring beauty and the complex life systems that exist in reefs under the water, I also frustratingly discovered that my capacity to enjoy that world was limited by the volume of air my lungs were able to hold. Snorkeling became an all-time favorite pastime after I was introduced to it. And, yet, I still felt shortchanged every time I had to surface to take a fresh breath of air. Then, several years ago I was introduced to scuba-diving equipment and trained in its use. With that equipment, and the training I

---

[42] Stephen Bevans, "God Inside Out: Toward a Missionary Theology of the Holy Spirit," *International Bulletin of Missionary Research* 22, no. 3 (1998).

received, I was able to immerse myself for hours in the underwater world by which I was so fascinated. What a difference this new equipment made, allowing me to explore and enjoy this other world hidden beneath the surface. In light of this discovery, I often now reflect with lament on the plight of a church constrained by the human capacities and limitations of its members. We are unable to go deep and enjoy the fullness of what God intends for us because we do not have the equipment that will fit us for God's purposes in us and through us. Just as I was liberated into a long enjoyment of the underwater world that I so loved through the equipment I was able to access, I believe the church can be liberated to become all that God intends us to be and to do through our immersion in the Spirit of God.

In a sermon to the Sanhedrin just before his death, Stephen, the first martyr, laments the problem of these religious leaders which he sees as preventing them from entering into the promises of God. He names their problem thus: "You always resist the Holy Spirit" (Acts 7:51). What an indictment! What if this indictment applied to our church also? This much seems clear from studying the role of the Holy Spirit in the mission with which the church has been entrusted: the measure of our effectiveness in mission, and of our faithfulness as disciples, is the measure of our submission to the Holy Spirit. I am convinced that the future vitality and thriving of the global Anabaptist family will be directly correlated with our ability to welcome the Holy Spirit and cultivate an anticipation of the work of the Holy Spirit among us. For the life and health of our congregations, we must choose whether we will value management strategies parroted from the secular corporate world or alternatively quick-fix techniques that seem to hold out hope but which have instead squandered the hopes of so many. Or, will we acknowledge our human limitations and frailties and welcome the work of God's Spirit into our lives and into our churches? The Brazilian missiologist, Valdir Steuernagel, framed this invitation in memorable words when he said: "Mission understood in pneumatological language is one act with two steps. It is first to perceive the blowing of the Spirit and the direction from which it comes. And then it is to run in the same direction to which the Spirit is blowing."[43]

## *STUDY QUESTIONS*

1. An important dimension of Christian growth is to consciously choose to rely on the Holy Spirit to guide our thoughts and actions (Rom6:11–14). Is the chief reason for our ineffectiveness in mission a breakdown in our reliance on the Holy Spirit for guidance and equipping in our call to be witnesses?

2. One of the key competencies in mission is learning how to track the where the Spirit is at work and joining in with what God is already doing. Do you agree? If so, what disciplines should we cultivate?

3. Could the widespread apathy towards mission and our faltering efforts or joylessness in our engagement in kingdom witness be an indication of the church's failure to discern and walk in the Spirit? What should change?

---

[43] Quoted in Samuel Escobar, *The New Global Mission: The Gospel from Everywhere to Everyone* (Downers Grove: InterVarsity Press, 2003), 127.

# Chapter 4

# The message of the gospel

## Antonio González

> **MESSAGE**
> We invite all people to acknowledge Jesus as
> Lord, turn from sin, receive baptism upon
> confession of faith and follow him in life as part
> of the worshipping, serving community of faith.
> This community is itself a sign to the world.
> We announce God's kingdom by serving others
> with humility and gratitude, caring for creation
> and seeking to live in the world without
> conforming to the powers of evil.

## INTRODUCTION

The message that the Christian community announces is the "gospel" of Jesus the Messiah ("Christ"). "Gospel" is possibly one of the words most used by Christians, to the point that many Protestants, not only conservatives, define themselves as "evangelicals." On the other hand, Catholic monks and nuns understand that their life is characterized by the "evangelical counsels."

## 1. WHAT IS THE GOSPEL?

Now, what is the gospel? What exactly is it about? When we ask these questions, we do not always get a clear answer.

For the medieval church, the "evangelical counsels" would be defined by the imitation of Jesus, and would be summarized in poverty, chastity, and obedience, typical of "religious life." Luther the monk protested against this understanding of the gospel. The gospel is not a model to be followed, but the "good news" *(euaggelion)* of the justification of the ungodly by faith alone, apart from the deeds of the law. It is not something else that we have to do (bad news), but the proclamation of what Jesus already did for us on the cross.[44]

Nowadays, some Christians would define the gospel as a system of values, and Jesus would be the model of those values. Everything related to love, peace, justice, equality, etc., would be, in some way "evangelical." For other Christians, however, the gospel would be a purely spiritual message. Sometimes this message is summarized in the "four spiritual laws," which talk about the love of God, the sin of human beings, the redeeming death of Christ, and salvation made possible through the accepting belief in this message.

All of these ideas have some truth to them. However, none of them fully reflects what Scripture calls gospel.

Of course, here it could be argued that the Scriptures themselves do not seem very unanimous in their presentation of the gospel. On one hand, the four "Gospels" speak repeatedly about the "gospel of the kingdom," which summarizes and characterizes the message of Jesus himself and his disciples (Matt 4:23; 9:35; 24:14; Mark 1:15; Luke 4:43; 8:1; Acts 8:12). On the other hand, in the epistles, especially in the Pauline epistles, we are told of a gospel that is more about Jesus and includes his death "for our sins" (1 Cor 15:1–3). So, are there several gospels? And what about

---

[44] "The main part and the basis of the Gospel is to accept Christ before taking him as an example" see M. Lutero, *Antología* (Barcelona: Producciones Editoriales del Nordeste, 1968), 85.

the Pauline warning that calls for anyone who preaches another gospel to be accursed (Gal 1:8–9)?

## 2. THE GOSPEL OF GOD

To order our thoughts on this matter, it is useful to begin by remembering the context in which the term gospel was used by the ancient world. The "good news," proclaimed by a herald, could announce the arrival of a victorious army, or of a man who came to govern a town. These connotations of "gospel" appeared already in ancient texts[45] and we also find them in the Greek translation of the famous Isaiah passage where the messenger appears on the mountains announcing the good news *(euaggelizomenou)* that God is coming to reign (Isa 52: 7 LXX).

In this reign of God, while we see a similarity with the "good news" of the ancient world, there is also an important difference. For Israel, the good news is that God himself reigns, instead of the reign of *other* lords. This is just one of the essential meanings of the Exodus narrative: God brought his people out from under Pharaoh's sovereignty to reign forever and ever (Exod 15:18). This entails a radical difference from the myths. In the mythical legitimations of rulers, we do not see God's direct reign, but rather a series of characters, like kings, who "reflect" on earth the sovereignty of God and are thus divinely justified.

As an alternative, Israel maintained a critical view of any monarchy other than the reign of God, including the failed monarchies of Israel and Judah: if God reigns, it makes no sense for others to reign. The reign of God is exclusive (this is what God's "jealousy" means). And precisely because it is exclusive, the reign of God creates a people of equals. If God

---

[45] Homer, *Odyssey* 14, 152. Available at: http://classics.mit.edu/Homer/odyssey.14.xiv.html. (Accessed: 7/10/2017).

is king, having other kings is treason (1 Sam 8, 12). If God is Lord, it makes no sense to have other lords. If God is a master, slavery is seriously questioned, making it practically a kind of "unemployment insurance" (Lev 25:53–55). If God is a warrior, there is no point in preparing for war, because he fights his people's battles (Exod 14:14, Deut 17:14–16, etc.).

In short, God reigns *directly* over his people, without intermediaries. And since the reign is direct, God has a monopoly on the roles of domination, excluding them from his people.

Now, we can understand better that Jesus' message about the imminent arrival of God's reign is a "gospel." The message of Jesus is "the gospel of God" (Mark 1:14), precisely because it announces that *God comes to reign*. The good news is that other kings, lords, masters and landowners are no longer going to exert their dominion over the people of God. This is the case because God himself, the true owner of the people and the earth (something emphasized by Jesus in his parables) comes to take back his lordship, rejecting the unjust domination of those who have taken over a people and a land that does not belong to them (Matt 12:1–12). In this way, the program of equality and justice outlined in the Torah will be completely and overwhelmingly accomplished, to the very last "dot" (Matt 5:18).

It is important to note that the reign of God breaks in freely, not by virtue of any merit of the people, as if they had obtained forgiveness through the expiatory sacrifices made in the temple. Quite the contrary: what has happened is that God, freely and sovereignly, has desired to come and reign, surpassing by his own generous initiative any obstacle that prevented his arrival. This reign comes already in the healings and deliverances carried out by Jesus (Matt 12:28), and it is received it a childlike way, taking joy in and practicing the same generous gratuity that God has displayed with his people. It is truly good news.

### 3. THE THREE ELEMENTS OF THE GOSPEL

What happens then with the gospel of Paul? Is it "another" gospel? There is only one passage in which Paul summarizes in some details the contents of the gospel that he proclaimed in the different communities (1 Cor 15:1–2). There we find three essential elements:

First, the gospel announces that the Messiah died for our sins in accordance with the Scriptures (1 Cor 15:3).

Second, the Messiah was raised on the third day in accordance with the Scriptures (1 Cor 15:4). In this second point, Paul draws out the argument because he wants to address this with the Corinthians, among whom were divergent opinions about the resurrection, possibly due to the dualistic tendencies of Greek culture (1 Cor 15:5–23).

Now Paul, while emphasizing the *real* nature of the resurrection, goes into the third element of the gospel, and which is a consequence of the previous one. What the gospel affirms is that Jesus, the Messiah, now carries out the sovereignty of God's reign. The entire human history has a meaning, which is the definitive manifestation of that sovereignty, displacing all forms of domination (1 Cor 15:24–28).

In the repeated expositions of the early Christian proclamation in the book of Acts, we find over and over these three elements: death, resurrection and proclamation of the sovereignty of the Messiah.[46] This is not something exclusive to Paul, although the sovereignty of Jesus is expressed in different forms, according to the context. For the Jews, Jesus is presented mainly as the Messiah (Acts 2:22–32), an

---

[46] See Acts 2:22-32; 3:12-26; 4:8-12; 5:31-32; 10:34-43; 13:16-41; 17:31.

expression that in a way summarizes Christian preaching (Acts 5:42). But Jesus is also presented as *the* definitive prophet (Acts 3:12–26), as the cornerstone and sole bearer of salvation (Acts 4:8–12), as prince and deliverer (Acts 5:31–32), or as "son of God" (Acts 13:16–41), in the sense of the messianic descendant of David, just as Nathan's prophecy had been interpreted (2 Sam 7:14). To the Gentiles, Jesus is presented as the definitive and universal "Judge" (Acts 10:34–43, 17:31). However, the basic structure of the three elements of the gospel remains constant.

It is important to point out the relevance of the second element of the gospel for the third: the early Christians interpreted the resurrection of Jesus as a messianic designation. God had declared Jesus as the son of God "by the resurrection from the dead" (Rom 1:4). Thereby, Jesus would be seated "at the right hand of God" (Rom 8:34), according to the model of Ps 110. Jesus is thus placed alongside the throne of God, a position to which neither the angels nor the patriarchs could come near.[47] Not only that. In some biblical images, there is not even talk of two thrones, but only one, belonging to God and to the Lamb (Rev 22:3).

## 4. ONE SINGLE REIGN

This image of Jesus at the right hand of the throne of God, or of a single throne, is decisive, because it presents us with a single reign of God, which is now carried out by the Messiah. It is necessary to take into account this fact, because some deeply rooted theological prejudices prevent us from grasping the singularity of God's reign. It is not that Jesus announced the reign of God, understood as an ethical utopia

---

[47] See R. Bauckham, *Monoteísmo y cristología en el Nuevo Testamento* (Terrasa: Clie, 2003), 28–30.

in the style of the Kantian "kingdom of ends," and that, later, early Christianity announced Jesus as "Christ," meaning some kind of mystical figure or celestial condition.[48] What happens is that there is still only one kingdom, the reign of God, and Jesus, as Messiah, is the "anointed" King to reign. That is precisely what the "Messiah" or "Christ" means.

Precisely because of this, the reign of God and the messiahship of Jesus do not refer to two different sovereignties, but to one single reign. This singularity of the reign of God is what the book of Acts expresses beautifully when at the end of it we see Paul who, in his "house arrest" in Rome, dedicates himself to proclaim "the reign of God and everything concerning the Lord Jesus the Messiah" (Acts 28:31) to all who visit him. Jesus, as Messiah, is king, and his reign is the reign of God. It is one single reign, carried out historically by the Messiah, who will abolish every dominion, every authority and every power, to finally deliver the kingdom to the Father, "that God be all in all" (1 Cor 15: 24–28).

In other words: precisely because there are not two reigns, there are not two gospels. Evidently, the condition for the unity of a single reign was the inclusion of Jesus in the divinity of the one God. And this also allows us to understand something often obscured by theological prejudices. Due to the speculations of Greek ontology, the affirmation of the divinity of the Messiah does not appear in Christian thought in a later form. The dynamics of and motives for including the

---

[48] The famous phrase of A. Loisy, according to which *Jésus annonçait le royaume, et c'est l'Église que est venue*, did not want to underline a discontinuity between the announcement of Jesus and Christianity, but quite the contrary, see A. Loisy, *L'Évangile et l'Église* (Paris: Alphonse Picard et Fils, 1902), 111.

Messiah in the monotheism of God are much earlier, and much more Jewish.

What the original Christian claim (about the inclusion of Jesus in the divinity of the one God intended) was precisely to sustain, in consonance with the Old Covenant, the *direct* reign of God. And this implies, as we saw before, the exclusion of intermediaries who could exercise the reign other than God would mean the introduction of new forms of domination, legitimized by being reflections of the heavenly divinity. It is not about saying that Jesus was another god, proclaiming another gospel, but rather including him in the *Shema* of Israel, to affirm a single and exclusive lordship (1 Cor 8:5–6)[49].

In reality, only the existence of the direct reign of God could be true to the prophets' preaching and to Jesus' proclamation of the breaking in of the exclusive reign of God. For this reason, the risen one could not be considered as an intermediate being, neither divine nor human. A Messiah who did not belong to the divinity of the one God would deny the direct reign of God, and thereby nullify the very preaching of Jesus. Because of this, Jesus' messiahship is understandable only after the resurrection, and *because of this* the gospel includes the resurrection of Jesus, and *therefore* any "other" gospel betrays the very idea of the coming of the direct reign of God.

It is significant that the so-called "unorthodox Judaeo-Christianity" (which refused to include Jesus in the divinity of the one God) not only made the Messiah a kind of angel,

---

[49] See Deut 6:4–5. Precisely the early use of expressions referring to God as *Kyrios* in the LXX to refer them to Jesus (Rom 10:13), or other issues related to the reign of God, in which it is outlined the belonging of Jesus to the monotheism of God (Heb 1:8, etc.).

but ended up accepting a whole plethora of intermediate beings in an ontological cascade more characteristic of Greek popular culture than of biblical revelation.[50] Affirming Jesus as Messiah, and affirming at the same time, and with Jesus, the *direct* government of God implies placing Jesus in the monotheism of God. Therefore, the divinity of Jesus begins to be affirmed very early, and in a very Hebrew context, before any metaphysical Greek speculation.

## 6. THE GOSPEL OF JESUS

We can thus understand the good news of the gospel in its New Testament unity: the reign of God has broken into history, and Jesus reigns as Messiah. The "gospel of God" (Rom 1:1; Mark 1:14) is the "gospel of the reign of God" (Mark 1:15), and it is the "gospel of Jesus the Messiah" (Mark 1:1).

The four canonical Gospels are then true gospel, not only because they expose the way God became King[51] again, but also because they show us who the King is, and how he reigns.

In the Old Covenant, God had exclusively assumed roles of domination, such as king, master or warrior, to exclude or limit those roles in the people of God. Jesus had added to this exclusivity the role of Father and the role of God as true owner of the earth, precisely to make known an Israel of brotherhood, without patriarchy or landlords (Matt 23: 9, Mark 10:30, Mark 12:1–11). Now then, if Jesus belongs to the monotheism of God, the gospel message shows us the true face of that God. The king is a servant, the master is a slave,

---

[50] See. H. J. Schoeps, *Theologie und Geschichte des Judenchristentums* (Tübingen: Mohr, 1949), 71–116; J. Daniélou, *Teología del judeocristianismo* (Madrid: Cristiandad, 2004), 77–123.
[51] See N. T. Wright, *How God Became King. Getting to the Heart of the Gospels* (New York: SPCK, 2012).

the warrior is a lamb, the landowner is a "carpenter," and the father is a brother. The King is human, and he is human to the point of death, even death on a cross.

The canonical Gospels are therefore then inseparable from the only gospel: through the stories about the life and the message of Jesus, we can know the true face of the Lord who comes to reign. It also follows that the "Sermon on the Mount" is inseparable from the only gospel, for as such we can know what is the "political program" of the King, the founding charter of his reign (Matt 5–7).

The Anabaptists, before the magisterial reformers, insisted on the utter impossibility of separating Jesus' practice and message from the announcement of the gospel. It is impossible to proclaim the reign without introducing the King. However, all this does not eliminate the importance of the first element of the gospel: the death of that King "for our sins." In fact, without this element of the gospel, nothing else is possible.

### 7. THE STRUCTURE OF THE FAILURE

In order to correctly understand the death of the Messiah "for our sins," it is necessary to understand what sin is. Sin is not a mere "transgression" of a norm, or a moral mistake. In the biblical sense, to sin is to "fail" in the sense of "missing the mark" *(khatta't, hamartía)*.

We could say that "missing the mark" has two fundamental elements: first, human beings do not place their trust in God as the possible foundation for life, but rather trust in creatures. They reject God. Secondly, by doing this, they attempt to base their own lives ("to eat") on the results ("fruits") of their own actions (Gen 3). It is self-foundation or self-justification.

As we know, "Adam" means "human being." The biblical account does not intend to talk about one particular person, but rather about what happens to every human being "from his youth" (Gen 8:21). Sin is a universal structure (Rom 3:23, 5:12).

Not only that, sin is expressed in multiple concrete manifestations: mutual distrust (Gen 3:7), using one another to get better results (Gen 3:16), fear of the God who evaluates what I produce (Gen 3:8), competition with God (Gen 11:1–9), competition with others (Gen 4: 1–5), religiosity that offers unsolicited sacrifices, envy, violence (Gen 4:1–8). Sin also results in guilt for what has been done (Gen 4:13) and an unmeasured anxiety to produce more and more, until the effort to produce curses the earth and ends in an ultimate and paradoxical outcome that lacks even a sense of self-justification: death (Gen 3:17–19).

There is another dimension of sin: the genesis of the "powers." To not believe God is always to believe in another creature, however creepy it may be, which promises to guarantee a connection between actions and results. This is what all powers do, be they religious, economic, social or political. In believing in them, the powers are magnified: the serpents become dragons (Rev 12:9, 20:2).

One example is the state. The first murderer founded the first city, that is, the first type of State (Gen 4:17), perhaps aspiring to stop the spiral of violent retribution (Gen 4:23–24). However, the State ends up being an empire. And the empire could be seen as the maximum expression of human sin, because in it we see the culmination of competition with God, domination of one another, idolatry of our own technical forces, and environmental abuse (Gen 11:1–9).

If sin consists in the logic of self-justification, then it is impossible to free oneself. If we liberated ourselves, such deliverance would be a merit of our own; therefore, we would ultimately remain prisoners of the same logic, boasting in the results of our own actions. This is symbolized by the sword that prevents the return to paradise (Gen 3:24).

## 8. THE GOOD NEWS OF THE LIBERATION

Despite the impossibility of saving ourselves, freedom from sin is not beyond our reach (Rom 10:8), rather it happens through the gospel. The gospel proclaims the death of the Messiah on the cross. Now, if the reign is one, and if the King is one, what the "word of the cross" affirms is the extraordinary fact that God himself was in the Messiah reconciling the world to himself (2 Cor 5:19).

Why reconciling? First of all, the cross shows the confrontation between God and sin. The idea of self-justification through the results of one's actions interprets all misfortune as the responsibility of the victim himself (John 9:2). It is the ultimate legitimization of the established order. But that same logic therefore declares that Jesus deserves his destiny, and he is an "accursed" rejected by God (Gal 3:13, Isa 53:4).

Now, if God was in Christ, he has radically confronted the retributive scheme that condemns him, rejecting "the charge of our legal indebtedness, which stood against us and condemned us" (Col 2:14). God has carried sin, that is, the rejection of God, but has forgiven instead of punishing. The logic of retribution has been destroyed on the cross. God does not validate retributive logic, but instead takes on himself all the consequences of retribution. Retribution, far from being the final structure on which we can found our praxis, is an enemy of God, the true foundation of our lives.

Hence, one immediate effect: the powers have lost their power, for the triumphant Messiah has made a public spectacle of them (Col 2:15). As we saw, the powers exist because they present themselves as, and are believed to be, a way of assuring the connection between certain actions and their results. If God, as the true foundation of our lives, is incompatible with retributive logic, the powers are deprived of their deep structure. The gospel that proclaims Jesus as Lord also proclaims the approaching end of all powers, because the foundation they offer is deceptive and apparent.

Ultimately, reconciliation happens because the ultimate structure of the rejection of God has been nullified, and because the powers which had taken over creation have been deprived of their strength, so that the Messiah has inaugurated his reign, which is the reign of God.

## 9. THE GOSPEL OF THE JUSTICE OF GOD

This means that the gospel is a manifestation of the God's justice (Rom 1:17). But in the biblical sense, justice (*sédeq*) does not have the sense of retribution as the Greek expression for which it was sometimes translated (*díke*). Many presentations of the gospel have projected on God a Greek idea of justice as retribution, which is more typical of Adam's sin than of the authentic justice of God.

In Scripture, justice is fidelity to the given word, fulfilment of commitments and, especially, faithfulness to the covenant. That is exactly why God can be just and, at the same time, forgive. Biblically, forgiveness is justice, since forgiveness consists precisely in the fact that God remains faithful to the covenant even when the other party has already broken it and, therefore, his obligations could be terminated (Dan 9:16, Esd 9:15; Isa 30:18, etc.). So forgiveness is an act of extreme justice, that is, faithfulness to the covenant which is extreme, freely given and undeserved.

This is so that the definitive and renewed covenant of God with his people would be a covenant in which God fulfils his promises and forgets all offenses. Precisely by nullifying the retributive logic, God shows himself to be just and forgiving of everyone who would accept forgiveness. God is just to forgive (1 John 1:9). In the same way, the justice of God manifested in Jesus, puts an end to all sacrifices, which are ultimately based on the logic of retribution.

The justice of God does not mean that God is driven by the Greek justice of retribution and cannot forgive without punishing someone. The justice of God means that God is characterized by such fidelity to his covenant that he forgives to the full extent even the gravest offenses, because the love that constitutes it abounds in grace upon grace. As Jesus explains, the justice of God produces a covenant equality, unlike retributive justice, which retains the logic of "Adam" and only causes inequality (Matt 20:1–16).

## 10. RECEIVING THE GOSPEL

At this point, it is clear that receiving the gospel consists in receiving Jesus, and in receiving him as Lord (Rom 10:13). It is not something we can do by our strength, but it is the work of the Holy Spirit in us. Without the Spirit you cannot proclaim Jesus as Lord (1 Cor 12:3). And yet, this receiving is free, and it is exceedingly so, because precisely where the Holy Spirit is there is freedom (2 Cor 3:17).

We could say that this receiving of the gospel of the Messiah, this invoking the name of the Lord (Acts 2:21) takes the form of three fundamental steps: repentance, baptism and the receiving of the Holy Spirit (Acts 2:38).

In the first place, what it is usually translated as "repentance" originally designated a "change of mind," and it is in a way the beginning of the complete "regeneration" of the human being. It is certainly true that the gospel proclaims the cancellation of the retributive logic on the cross, and therefore the complete forgiveness of God, independent of all sacrifices. This is something that happens totally independently from us. However, when we believe the gospel, a new birth begins immediately. Jesus not only forgives sins, but he also frees us from sins (Matt 1:21, Acts 3:26, etc.).

And, to the extent that we believe God was in Christ reconciling the world to himself, to that same extent we are also freed, through the Spirit, from our claim to self-justification. In other words, insofar as we trust in the God revealed in Jesus, we are freed from the deep structure of sin, and a transformation takes place in us. Instead of pursuing our own way, "we are converted" (Matt 18: 3), that is, God turns us toward himself as one who is trustworthy, unlike all the powers of this world.

Second, in baptism the transformation of our being transpires in the likeness of the death and resurrection of Jesus (Rom. 6:1–11). The old man, its distrust of God, its efforts at self-foundation, and all its concrete expressions are submerged in the waters, to emerge to the new life. More than a "symbol", baptism is a symbolic *action*, which comes through the identification of the believer with Jesus, so that our spirit participates in the same movement of the Spirit that raised him from the dead (Rom 8:11)[52].

Third, being filled with the Holy Spirit. Indeed, neither faith nor the gift of repentance (John 16: 8, Acts 11:18, etc.), nor baptism are possible without the Spirit. That said, the entire Christian life can be defined as "always being filled with the Spirit," which is precisely what the present passive imperative of Eph 5:18 expresses. The "fullness", far from being a one-time thing, is a permanent experience in the

---

[52] See P. Marpeck, *The Writings of Pilgram Marpeck*, ed. W. Klaassen and W. Klaassen (Scottdale: Herald Press, 1978), 169–261.

Christian life (Acts 4:31), which manifests itself in several fundamental dimensions: freedom to bear witness (Acts 2:14–36), supernatural signs of the presence of the reign of God (Acts 3:1–10), and the formation of a fraternal community in which social differences disappear (Acts 2:43–47).

## CONCLUSION: THE NEW HUMANITY

In fact, the Christian community is a vital sign of the arrival of God's reign. Its very existence constitutes the recognition of the new sovereignty of God in the Messiah and therefore a decisive sign of the reality that the gospel announces. With its existence, the Christian community declares that another world is possible. But the existence of the Christian community is not possible without breaking the ties to the old systems of power: the announcing and denouncing also require renouncing.

In fact, the sovereignty of God only begins to be proclaimed when a people that breaks away from the sovereignty of this world's powers begins to exist. The powers are then confronted with a free community (Eph 3:10), which in this way gives testimony to the new world, to the new humanity. Such a humanity no longer believes in the powers of this world, nor needs them to justify itself, nor conforms to them, nor originates new powers, because it is ruled directly by the Messiah.

Now the reign of God is a shared reign, in which all its members are invited to reign with the Messiah (Rom 5:17, 2 Tim 2:12, Rev 5:10). How can they all reign without anyone being a servant? How is it possible to overcome the secular differences between those who serve and those who are served? The Messiah gives us the solution: in a community in which everyone serves, everyone can at the same time be king (Luke 22:24–30). Such service is a gift of the Spirit, as it allows us to participate in the Spirit's very mission and can therefore only be done with humility and gratitude, free from any attempt at self-justification.

Thus appears a new humanity freed from the desire to produce results, and that is why it has a new way of relating to the rest of the creation. Creation certainly yearned for the manifestation of the true humanity (Rom 8:19), a humanity capable of taking care of the garden of God, instead of subjecting it to its unbridled logic of self-justifying production. This is the humanity that announces the message of the gospel, until all powers are deactivated, and God is all in all.

## STUDY QUESTIONS

1. What difference can you see between the ways the author explains the content of the gospel and traditional ways of understanding the gospel?
2. What does the gospel have to do with the reign of God?
3. What is the relation between the proclamation of the gospel and the powers of this world?
4. How does the gospel affect the future of the humanity?

# Chapter 5

# Scope and task of our mission

## GOING BEYOND OUR COMMUNITIES: INTO THE NOMADIC LAND OF MONGOLIA

Petrus Eko Handoyo

> ### SCOPE and TASK
> *We go beyond our communities as witnesses, following Jesus' instructions to make disciples of all peoples. We form new communities of believers, transcending boundaries of nationality, culture, class, gender and language. Because we believe that God has created and blessed cultural variety, we expect new forms of the church to emerge as we go.*

## INTRODUCTION

As the redeemed people of God,[53] we are deeply grateful that we are able to respond to the command of Jesus Christ to *go out* beyond our communities and to become witnesses for him alone. This is also the *choice* we have had, which truly comes from *freedom*. Here, Godself himself gives

---

[53] We may compare this with Titus 2:14; Gal 1:4, 3:14. Also, God *has chosen* us to be a people for his treasured possession that we should keep all his commands. More preciously, we may *declare* the praises of him to others. See in Deut 14:2, 26:18; 1 Pet 2:9; 2 Thess 2:13.

us the freedom to choose.[54] We, furthermore, are thought to be *responsible* for many of the things that we do. These are moral issues we may cope with in our everyday life.[55] When we choose to *go* beyond our communities, we then understand that it is indeed one of the most priceless spiritual blessings that come from our freedom of choice.

## 1. THE COMMAND TO GO AND TO BEAR FRUIT

The Gospel of John 15:16 points out that Jesus *chose* (Gr. *exelexamēn*) the disciples for a missional task. This is very crucial for the sending of the disciples to reach out the nations as well as people groups in many parts of the world (cf. John 4:36 in the context of missional outreach and 12:24 in the context of reaching the Greeks, and also Acts 1:8 in the context of being transformed witnesses). [56] Here, what Jesus said in John 15:16 basically has two parts: "*I* on my part chose *you* and appointed you, *etheka*, placed you in an important position."[57] It is obvious: believers sense an honour and also carry out the task to go out to various places that the Holy Spirit leads them for God's great work.[58]

---

[54] Cf. Gen 2:15–17. In the passage, God gave Adam *freedom* to *choose*. Adam was absolutely *free* to eat from any tree in the garden, except from the tree of knowledge of good and evil. He, moreover, *chose* wrongly.
[55] Freedom, choice and responsibility are the *basic* issues in moral philosophy (ethics) that influence our value judgment. For further discussion, see Petrus Eko Handoyo, *Exploring Values: An Analytical Study of the Philosophy of Value Axiology* (Saarbrücken: VDM GmbH & Co, 2011), 69.
[56] Cf. Ben Witherington, III, *John's Wisdom: A Commentary on the Fourth Gospel* (Louisville: Westminster John Knox Press, 1995), 257.
[57] Richard Charles H. Lenski, *The Interpretation of St. John's Gospel 11-21* (Minneapolis: Augsburg Fortress, 2008), 1052.
[58] David W. Shenk, "Gifts That Anabaptists Offer in Interfaith Encounter," in *Fully Engaged: Missional Church in an Anabaptist Voice*,

We may find this sending of the disciples into the world in John 15:16, 17:18, and 20:21.[59] Moreover, Hans Kasdorf[60] describes that the members of the believers' church in the New Testament tradition maintain their deep awareness of sentness for witness. Their sense of priority of the mission found expression not only in a conviction of being sent by the Lord Jesus, but also in a recognition of responsibility to send missionaries into all the world across social, cultural, linguistic, economic, religious and geographical frontiers. And in relation to our context here, what Kasdorf[61] states is right, "Mission always implies the crossing of frontiers from faith to unfaith."

Again, let us look into the phrase in John 15:16, "…you might go and bear fruit…" These words are interrelated. First, the mandate *to go* and *to bear fruit* in this verse is the climax of Jesus' teaching on the vine and the branches (15:1–17). It is completely intended for the believers to bear *witness* to the world, as well.[62] The Lord Jesus has chosen us *to go*, not as an end in itself, but in order that we may *produce* much fruit.

---

eds. Stanley W. Green and James R. Krabill (Harrisonburg & Kitchener: Herald Press, 2015), 254–255. Shenk notes several gifts that may characterize global Anabaptists as they bear witness among various religions in the world.

[59] Cf. Hans Burger, *Being in Christ: A Biblical and Systematic Investigation in a Reformed Perspective* (Eugene: Wipf & Stock, 2009), 373.

[60] Hans Kasdorf, "The Anabaptist Approach to Mission," in *Anabaptism and Mission*, ed. Wilbert R. Shenk (Scotdale: Herald Press, 1984), 69.

[61] Ibid; also cf. Calvin E. Shenk, "Essential Themes for an Anabaptist Missiology", in *A Relevant Anabaptist Missiology for the 1990s*, ed. Calvin E. Shenk (Elkhart: Council of International Ministries, 1990), 63.

[62] Cf. Ben Witherington, III, *John's Wisdom: A Commentary on the Fourth Gospel*, 257.

And here, we may *contribute* to the mission of the Christian community.[63]

Second, the command *to go* and *to bear fruit* is not only circumstantial. Yet, it really indicates the actual *going* of the apostolic mission, which Jesus does commission his disciples to carry to all parts of the world (Matt 28:19; Mark 16:15; Luke 24:48; John 20:19–23; Acts 1:8).[64] And, the results of 'going' and 'bearing fruit' should last. Nowadays, we have seen that we truly get involved in various missional ministries in many places in the world.

## 2. A NATION WITH A NOMADIC IDENTITY

As we respond to the command of our Lord Jesus Christ to go beyond our communities as witnesses to all nations and peoples, we then reach out to, for example, the nomadic land of Mongolia [65] in Central Asia. Mennonite Mission Network, formerly Mennonite Board of Missions, has carried out missional work in the country since 1993. God opened the door for our ministry in "the land of the blue sky" right after the Mongolian socialist system collapsed in 1992,

---

[63] Ibid., 260.

[64] Richard Charles. H. Lenski, *The Interpretation of St. John's Gospel 11–21*, 1052; also, Wilbert R. Shenk, *By Faith, They Went Out: Mennonite Missions, 1850–1999* (Elkhart: Institute of Mennonite Studies, 2000), 131.

[65] Over the past 24 years, Mennonite Mission Network has been in partnership with the Joint Christian Services International (JCSI, a consortium of denominational mission agencies) in Mongolia and also Mongolia Mission Partnership (MMP, a cluster of Mennonite churches in eastern Ohio) in the U.S. The Network sent Laura Schlabach as an earliest representative of the Mennonite church's desire to build the community of Jesus followers in Mongolia. See "Mongolia Partners: 20 years of sharing the Word through deeds," in *Beyond Ourselves*, October 2013, Vol. 12, No. 2, (2013), 3.

which later caused the new adoption of non-Soviet Constitution in the same year.

Here, an essential question may arise. What makes Mongolia truly unique among the world's nations? Mongolia always relates to the *nomadic* lifestyle.[66] This life style may have been long for centuries in the steppes as well as in the deserts. And until today, the Mongols carry on living their nomadic ways. Furthermore, the lifestyle also may give a sense of nomadic identity for this Central Asian nation. It becomes obvious that when the Mongols lose contact with their nomadic lifestyle, they may also lose their true identity.[67]

This distinctive identity can be traced back to the existence of the first steppe empire of Mongolia in 209 BC called the Hun Empire.[68] The empire itself was created under the charismatic leadership of *shanyu* (king) Modun. The Huns, therefore, may have been the present-day Mongol ancestors.

Another crucial attempt to maintain the nomadic identity among the Mongols was to establish the Great

---

[66] Petrus Eko Handoyo, *Panggilan Padang: Pengembaraan Misi ke dalam Kehidupan Nomaden Mongolia*, "Steppe Call: A Missional Journey into Mongolian Nomadic Life," (Yogyakarta: Penerbit Andi, 2016), 4–5, 41–42, 215–216; cf. Gaby Bamana, *On the Tea Road: A Journey into Mongolian Life and Culture* (Ulaanbaatar: Admon Publishing House, 2008), 14–16, 150–151; also Bat-Ochir Bold, *Mongolian Nomadic Society: A Reconstruction of the 'Medieval' History of Mongolia* (Richmond: Curzon Press, 2001), 3.

[67] Jane Blunden, *Mongolia* (Bucks: Bradt Guides, 2014), 103.

[68] It is also called the Hunnu or Xiongnu Empire, which dominated the entire Central Asia. It stretched from Korea to Lake Baikal in Siberia, and from south into northern China. Cf. Bat-Erdene Baabar, *History of Mongolia* (Ulaanbaatar: Nepko Publishing, 2006), 6; Christopher Pratt Artwood, *Encyclopedia of Mongolia and Mongol Empire* (Bloomington: Facts on File, 2004), vii–viii.

Mongol Empire, or *Ikh Mongol*. It was done by Chinggis Khaan[69] in 1206 after unifying the nomadic tribes in the surrounding Central Asian regions. [70] To the present day, he has been viewed as the founder of the Mongol identity,[71] as well.

Regarding the steppe nomads in Central Asia, another significant question may be raised here. In what main reason did the Chinese kings in ancient China establish the great fortifications (now the Great Wall of China with 21,196 kilometers long)[72] that stretched from east to west of their territories? By looking back at the regional history as early as the seventh century BC, some people may recognize that the Great Wall of China was mainly built because of nomads' attacks and invasions from the northern steppes and deserts.[73]

In relation to the Christian mission during the reigns of Mongol kings from the 12th to 14th centuries, Khubilai Khaan[74] (1260–1294) was considered more tolerant than his grandfather, Chinggis Khaan, and other kings. One of the reasons for his openness of religious affairs in the huge

---

[69] An alternate spelling is Genghis Khan.

[70] Ibid., 2006, 12; also, Jeremiah Curtin, *The Mongols: A History* (New York: Cosimo Classics, 2008), 4.

[71] Gaby Bamana, *On the Tea Road: A Journey into Mongolian Life and Culture*, 14; ibid., 2006, 13. Cf. Christopher P. Artwood, *Encyclopedia of Mongolia and Mongol Empire*, 365, 367.

[72] "China's Great Wall is Longer than Previously Thought," in *BBC News*, 6 June 2012. Available at: http://www.bbc.com/news/world-asia-china-18337039. (Accessed: 7/25/2017).

[73] Cf. Bat-Erdene Baabar, *History of Mongolia*, 6; Petrus Eko Handoyo, *Panggilan Padang: Pengembaraan Misi ke dalam Kehidupan Nomaden Mongolia*, "Steppe Call: A Missional Journey into Mongolian Nomadic Life," 11; Bat-Ochir Bold, *Mongolian Nomadic Society: A Reconstruction of the 'Medieval' History of Mongolia*, 3.

[74] An alternate spelling is Kublai Khan

Mongol empire was the influence of his mother, Sorghaghtani Beki, a Christian Nestorian from the Kereyid tribe.[75] Through her, Khubilai was then sympathetic to Christianity. Moreover, he was one of the most educated nomads[76] and also was a gifted warrior.[77]

One significant matter that Khubilai Khaan had done during his great imperial leadership, which also gives some missional *impact* on the world's Christian church history today, was to write a very special letter to the pope[78] in Rome, Italy. He made a request for the pope to send one hundred Christian missionaries to his Mongol court.[79] The purpose was to teach the Christian faith to the Mongol peoples. In 1271, Pope Gregory X, the newly elected pope, sent two Dominican missionaries together with Niccolò Polo, his brother Matteo Polo, and his son Marco Polo (1254–1324), who was around 17 years old, to the Mongol court in the Far East. The papacy also provided his missionaries with jewels

---

[75] Denis C. Twitchett and Herbert Franke, *The Cambridge History of China: Alien Regimes and Border States 907–1368*, Vol. 6 (Cambridge: Cambridge University Press, 1994), 414; cf. Robert Marshall, *Storm from the East: From Ghengis Khan to Khubilai Khan* (Berkeley & Los Angeles: University of California Press, 1993), 194–195.

[76] Bat-Erdene Baabar, *History of Mongolia*, 18.

[77] Robert Marshall, *Storm from the East: From Ghengis Khan to Khubilai Khan*, 195.

[78] The pope was Pope Clement IV and then died in 1269 when Niccolò Polo and his brother Matteo Polo with Khubilai Khaan's letter in hands arrived at the port of Acre, on the eastern Mediterranean coast, close to home in Venice. Tim McNeese, *Marco Polo and the Realm of Kublai Khan* (Philadelphia: Chelsea House Publishers, 2006), 39. Cf. Bailey Wallys Diffie and George D. Winius, *Foundations of the Portuguese Empire 1414–1580* (Minneapolis: University of Minnesota Press, 1977), 19.

[79] Christopher Pratt Artwood, *Encyclopedia of Mongolia and Mongol Empire*, 438; ibid., 1977; Jane Blunden, *Mongolia*, 100.

and other items to give to Khubilai Khaan as gifts. On the coast of Cilicia in Lesser Armenia, the Polos, two missionaries, and others on the caravan faced a threat from the local ruler.[80] Eventually, the two missionaries decided to turn back to Rome. The Polos would then continue on with no single missionary or representative of the pope.[81] Concerning this, another question may again be asked here. What missional impact would be on the Christianity today if *one hundred missionaries* were truly sent out to serve the Mongol empire since the thirteenth century?

### 3. BEING GRATEFUL FOR WHAT WE HAVE

The book of 1 Kings 17:7–16 gives us a significant outlook, which may be *similar* to our missional context in Mongolia. The prophet Elijah truly had a single-minded commitment to God. He was the most dramatic and most famous prophet in Israel during the period of the divided kingdom. Moreover, he chose to carry out his work for God and underwent great isolation from others for several years in the desert, east of the Jordan River.[82]

The Lord then commanded Elijah to go to Zarephath, a coastal town between Sidon and Tyre in the land of Phoenicia. There was a poor widow who would supply the prophet with food from what she had. The woman and her son were facing starvation because there had been no rain for a

---

[80] The local ruler here was the Sultan of Egypt. He had invaded Armenian territory and attacked Christian communities and towns. The safety was the main concern for the Polos, the missionaries, and some of others as they were also Christians. Tim McNeese, *Marco Polo and the Realm of Kublai Khan*, 48–49.

[81] Ibid., 49.

[82] In 1 Kings 17:2 and 5, the Lord had told the prophet Elijah to go to the Kerith Ravine, east of the Jordan River, and stayed there.

long time. She herself seemingly had a pagan background.[83] In verse 13, Elijah's request for a small loaf of bread is actually a *test* of the woman's faith. It says, "… But first make a small cake of bread for me from what you have[84] and bring it to me, and then make something for yourself and your son".

> Here it is apparent, the prophet Elijah asked the widow to give him the bread from what she had, not from what she did not have. The prophet might know about her existential condition as she and her boy lived in the dry land. In the midst of her hard life, the ordinary woman was pleased to share the bread with the prophet Elijah from what she had. Furthermore, the Bible says, "It is more blessed to give than to receive" (Acts 20:35).

So often, in our spiritual journey, God wants us to give to his service *from what we have*, not from what we do not have. What do we want to offer to God anyway? Here, we may offer him our abilities, talents, values, gifts, commitment, as well as experiences in spite of the difficulties and limitations we would encounter. Above all, we may give our life to him.

Jaal, 73 years old, was a grandmother and also a church leader. Despite her advanced age, she was willing to serve a smaller congregation in Ikhkhet *sum* (town).[85] This small

---

[83] See Luke 4:25–26.

[84] We may find a similar phrase "from what you have" in 2 Kgs 4:2; Mark 6:38; Matt 15:34; Acts 3:6. Also cf. Heb 13:5.

[85] Every spring, Union Bible Theological College (UBTC) in Ulaanbaatar, Mongolia, sends out a number of students for around two weeks for some

town with around 2,000 people, is very remote and dusty. It is located in Dornogovi province in the southeastern part of the Gobi Desert. The congregation uniquely met in a *ger*, a Mongolian round, felt tent. And this is *Zalbirliin Orgoo* (Palace of Prayer), a kind of a house church, where some nomadic families also attended the Sunday worship service.

When the congregation got together in the first year, Jaal considered that one of several men should take a lead, not an old woman like her. She, at first, thought that Mukhjargal might be their leader. He had attended the worship services regularly. And, he was in his forties with 5 children. Yet, the great obstacle blocked the congregation's decision. It was because Munkhjargal was a nomad. From Monday to Friday, he spent the most of his time in the vast steppe-desert. His wife Delgermaa faithfully helped him live the harsh nomadic life. On the weekends, they returned home to see their children[86] in Ikhkhet town. His wife sometimes went home

---

missional evangelistic trips to the countryside and smaller towns throughout the country. The purpose is to help the countryside churches and also to reach out the unbelievers both in the steppes as well as the deserts. Each team is always accompanied by a lecturer, either Mongolian or missionary. I had great opportunities to accompany my students to go out to a number of isolated places in the deserts and the steppes during my five-year teaching assignment at UBTC, including to Ikhkhet located in the middle of nowhere in the Gobi Desert. These were so precious missional trips for me to see the peoples praising God and singing for joy because of his blessings (cf. Ps 67). In this place, together with the local congregation, we also served the nomadic families in the surrounding deserts. Many of UBTC students who joined me on the missional trips had received student aid from Schowalter funds through Mennonite Mission Network.

[86] While the nomadic families live their harsh nomadic life in the deserts as well as the steppes, they also pay great attention to their children's education. A number of families send their children to go to the

earlier. At the same time, their relatives helped take care of their livestock.

Although Jaal was an unschooled, ordinary woman, she and the congregation had great courage to preach the good news of salvation to their community and beyond as the transforming power of the Holy Spirit enabled them (cf. Acts 4:13). Together, they also encouraged four Sunday school teachers,[87] who were teenagers, to reach out to other kids in their surrounding districts. Those teenagers actively got involved in the evening prayer meeting and Sunday service, as well.

On Easter Sunday, those teenagers and some church members held a special celebration by inviting many other kids beyond their community. Surprisingly, there were sixty kids and teenagers attending the service. The *ger*, the tent they usually met and worshipped in together, could not accommodate the larger number of kids and teens that morning. Immediately, they made a crucial decision by holding the particular meeting outside of the *ger*. It now became an outdoor Easter service in the desert town. It was so lovely and blessed! Above them, the sky was blue and clear. And the desert wind blew gently.

For the congregation, it was apparent, they truly wanted to share their Christian values as well as life experiences with people in their communities *from what they had* in spite of

---

countryside schools in the nearby towns. Some children may stay at the school dormitories and some may stay with their relatives. Yet, in many situations, children may prefer to stay at the dormitories. Here in Ikhkhet town, there is also a boarding school for many nomad children.
[87] Ryan Miller, *In Mongolia, Mennonite = Ministry*, in *Mennonite Mission Network News*, Wednesday, August 26, 2009. Available at: https://www.mennonitemission.net/news/In%20Mongolia,%20Mennonite %20=%20ministry. (Accessed: 7/08/2017).

their limitations they encountered. Furthermore, their leap of faith in the Spirit of Jesus, which makes it possible for committed followers to be transformed,[88] was to lead the local people to know more about the wonderful work of God. The people also might realize, through their witnesses, that the kingdom of God is near (cf. Matt 3:2, 4:17; Mark 1:15; Luke 16:16, 17:20–21).

Neemekh, the regent of Ikhkhet town, was an unbeliever. He had responded to the Christianity positively as he knew the existence of the Zalbirliin Orgoo Church, the only one in his region. A Mongolian believer once gave him the Bible as a gift. The regent told us that he had not found any false teachings in it. Even though some people might have some negative viewpoint on Christianity, Neemekh himself had seen the good programs that the local congregation did for the spiritual renewal to the communities.

### 4. GOD HAS BLESSED CULTURAL VARIETY

We believe that our living God has created and also blessed cultural variety with a very particular purpose. Regarding this, Brian M. Howell and Jenell Williams Paris note, "When God created humans in the garden, living in perfect unity with God and each other, they expressed that perfect unity in the cultural modes of language and culture. God does not redeem humanity by bringing us back together into a single language or culture. Instead, God blesses cultural diversity by sending the gospel out in the diverse languages

---

[88] Palmer Becker, "What is an Anabaptist Christian?" *Missio Dei* No 18 (Elkhart: Mennonite Mission Network, 2008), 7.

of the world. Diversity is not a curse, but a blessing to be encouraged, embraced, and enjoyed."[89]

Cultural diversity does not purposefully produce any conflict among the nations as well as peoples, although there might be different contexts and values. Here, we may experience God through any language or culture in it instead. Much of the Bible deals with issues connected to the interactions of diverse cultures. And it is amazing that God wants us to appreciate and to respect various languages and cultures among us as the blessings.[90] Moreover, in Lev 19:33–34, the Israelites are highly encouraged to treat an alien (a foreigner) justly when he lives with them in their land, and also love him as themselves. This is because the Israelites were also aliens in the land of Egypt. And, they *must* know that God also loves the aliens.

However, we may look into another Bible passage concerning the diversity in Psalm 67, too. It is called a missionary psalm.[91] Verses 3–7 tell us as to how the nations and the peoples of the earth have seen the majestic existence of God and also his great blessings among them. They would give praises to God alone and be glad and sing for joy, because God shall rule and guide them with just and equitable government. God would *lead* the nations and the peoples as he led the Israelites through the wilderness.[92] And, our God is a God for all nations and peoples on earth.

---

[89] Brian M. Howell and Jenell Williams Paris, *Introducing Cultural Anthropology: A Christian Perspective* (Grand Rapids: Baker Academic, 2011), 256.

[90] Cf. Patty Lane, *A Beginner's Guide to Crossing Cultures: Making Friends in a Multicultural World* (Downers Grove: InterVarsity Press, 2002), 138–139.

[91] Cf. James E. Smith, *The Wisdom Literature and Psalms* (Joplin: College Press Publishing Company, 2007), 319.

[92] Ibid., 320.

I had seen how God greatly blessed the four Mongolian churches with the cultural variety in Baruun Urt town, the capital of Sukhbaatar province, in the eastern Mongolia. Baruun Urt is an isolated town with around 15,000 people. Dominated by the flat steppe, it is located in the middle of nowhere. The local church leaders coming from the different cultural and ethnic backgrounds closely worked together with one purpose, that is, to preach the good news of Christ to their peoples and others. These four young leaders with the faithful hearts are truly willing to serve God and to build his kingdom in their communities and the surrounding steppes where the nomadic families lived their daily nomadic lives.

Enkhsaruul, in her thirties, pastored *Munkhiin Gegee* (Eternal Dawn) church. It was a house church, where the congregation met at a small wooden house. And together with two other church leaders, we visited two nomadic families in the steppes. They also attended the Sunday service at Enkhsaruul's church. One of them was Naraa. She was 24 years old. I saw the Mongolian Holy Bible on the table inside her *ger*, nomadic tent. She was born to a nomad girl in Sukhbaatar province and continues her nomadic life until today. For her, Jesus Christ is the Saviour and gives her a new life. We experienced a sweet fellowship with her and her family as they began to slaughter a very big sheep. Then, we all ate *khorkhog* (a Mongolian barbeque dish) outside of their *ger* and also enjoyed together the beauty of the blue sky in the lonely steppe.

Enkhsaruul was an open-minded leader. Also, she was willing to share her place of worship with another congregation, *Uurchlult* (Transformation), where Dugersuren was their leader. His congregation met at 2:00 p.m. He had some burden to reach out the youths through sports activities.

Another church leader, Nergui, too, made a good connection with Enksaruul, Dugersuren, and Munkhbat of *Avraliin Naran* (Sun of Salvation). Nergui, in his twenties, served *Tal Nutagiin Gerel* (Light of Steppe) a congregation that met at a smaller wooden house. The splendid thing here was that the four church leaders got together for a regular prayer meeting each month. And, these young leaders understood that the diversity among them and also the congregations was a great blessing to them all.

In the New Testament, we may also find similar interactions of various cultures as the apostles and believers sense the coming of the Holy Spirit on the day of Pentecost in Jerusalem. The Holy Spirit miraculously *touched* individuals, which had different languages and cultures at Pentecost (cf. Acts 2:1–4, 9–11). The Spirit absolutely enabled them to know more about the cultural variety among themselves.

As a matter of fact, the diversity itself has its main purpose for the communities of believers. The book of Acts frankly points out that the cultural differences may *declare the wonders of God in the different tongues*.[93] With the cultural diversity, we may also become witnesses as the chosen and redeemed people of God that we would declare the praises of God in our communities and beyond (cf. 1 Pet 2:9).[94] Again, God has affirmed the cultural variety as we *go out* and serve the nations and peoples in many different settings and contexts around the world.

---

[93] Acts 2:11 says, "… (both Jews and converts to Judaism); Cretans and Arabs—we hear them declaring the wonders of God in our own tongues!"
[94] 1 Pet 2:9 tells, "But you are a chosen people, a royal priesthood, a holy nation, God's special possession, that you may declare the praises of him who called you out of darkness into his wonderful light."

## STUDY QUESTIONS

1. Among a number of life choices, we have, as communities of believers, do we truly consider that choosing *to go* beyond our areas for God's missional task is desperately one of the most priceless spiritual blessings?[95]

2. Read Psalm 67 thoroughly. By looking into the story of Khubilai Khaan, have we ever seen any non-Christian ruler (local or national) in the modern times being so open to the gospel message and asking for more missionaries or Christian volunteers to serve in his or her territory but the churches as well as sending agencies are *reluctant* to respond to them? What meaningful lesson do we learn from these missional contexts?

3. The theme "from what we have" (cf. 1 Kgs 17:13)[96] is indeed an existential one. Whether a person is rich or poor, old or young, educated or unschooled, he or she absolutely has something to offer to God. In the midst of hardship or pleasantness, feeling unhappy or happy, have we ever felt hesitant to give our service to God as he is calling us to take part in his missional work? What is the true meaning *from what we have* for us as we respond to Jesus' missional command *to go out* and to serve the nations and the peoples around the world?

---

[95] Cf. John 15:16.
[96] Also see 2 Kgs 4:2; Mark 6:38; Matt 15:34; Acts 3:6; Heb 13:5.

4. God has really blessed cultural variety by sending the gospel out in various cultures as well as languages of the world. He really loves all nations and peoples on earth. Cf. Ps 67:3–7; Acts 2:11. Describe in your own context, either locally or nationally, as to how people respond to God has blessed cultural variety. Furthermore, explore whether cultural diversity is genuinely a blessing, a stumbling block or a curse.

# Chapter 6

# Risk and suffering

Victor Pedroza Cruz

> **RISK and SUFFERING**
> *We trust God in all areas of life, living as peacemakers who renounce violence, love our enemies, seek justice and focus especially on serving and reaching out to the weak, poor, vulnerable, voiceless and oppressed.*
> *Because Jesus Christ suffered for us, we also accept risk and suffering for his sake.*

## INTRODUCTION

The announcement of the good news, *the gospel*, involves new life, joy and consolation where there is weeping; joy where there is sadness; hope where it seems that everything is over. It entails reconciliation, fraternal relationships, love instead of hate, peace where there is war, salvation when it seems that everything is lost. However, it also involves risk, conflict and suffering. For example, when we announce the gospel, the powers (*exousiai*: principalities and authorities, powers and lordships – Eph 1:21, Col 1:15) are discovered and unmasked. The systems of iniquity (because they are impious and unjust) are confronted, bringing about risks and suffering for missionaries and emerging communities of believers.

As followers of Jesus, we announce freedom to alcoholics and drug addicts. We announce a dignified life and true love to all those who, out of necessity or not, prostitute themselves. We announce that marital harmony is possible and that the broken families can be restored. We bring doctors and medicines at no cost. We dress the poor, the needy and the destitute. We provide literacy and teach professions. Consequently, the powers[97] are alarmed: the people who sell drugs, the men who operate the brothels, the sorcerers and miracle charlatans, the pedophiles and other type of abusive adults. The traders of religious merchandise are alarmed. In addition, the doctors (who negotiate with human health), the pharmaceutical businesses, the bar owners and the drug house operators become worried. Abusive men are alarmed when the women respond with joy to the arrival of the Liberator. The "Casanovas" are alarmed when they learn that commitment, fidelity, love and forgiveness are real possibilities that can be lived. False religions that hold men, women and even children captive are challenged.

The gospel is the good news to the poor, healing to the broken-hearted, proclamation of freedom for the captives, sight for the blind, freedom for the oppressed, proclamation of the favourable year of the Lord (Luke 4:16–21). Consequently, anything different from this, then it is not gospel.

### 1. DISCIPLESHIP LESSONS

A very sad letter is sent from Rome to the community of believers in Philippi. The church is unhappy. Their apostle, their messenger, their herald is in prison. Why is he in prison? What did he do? What is he accused of? Paul himself answers, ". . . to advance . . . for the defence of the gospel" (Phil 1:12, 16) or in other words because he preached the good news of Jesus Christ, announcing that "there is another king . . . Jesus" (Acts 17:7).

---

[97] These are all those organized crime groups.

The very church in Philippi was born in a situation of conflict. The missionaries went in search of the devout Jewish women who gathered to pray. For this *new way* of life, women are valuable human beings in the eyes of God. But, there was another woman, a non-Jewish one, who was looking for God and who, impacted by the message, believed and was baptized. Then, she invited the disciples to her house and forced them to stay. Missionaries know what this is like: whenever we arrive, there is someone waiting. When they believe, they for sure will invite us to their house and force us to stay with them. This is how the church begins and because there is so much joy, we do not consider the risks.

The powers were then alarmed at the presence of the missionaries. As we can recall, the young woman, who was a slave of demons and slave of men who own her, was liberated. Moreover, the reactions from these men came swiftly, because now their profit would be gone. They realized that the gospel is another way of living and they say, "You are bringing some strange ideas to our ears, and we would like to know what they mean" (Acts 17:20). The violence of the masses was unleashed against the missionaries with the support and participation of the institution: they sent the missionaries into jail.

The story follows when we see that Paul and Silas sing. Then, the Holy Spirit pushed the door open to let them out. They preached to the guard. They baptized him and his family. The guard treats the wounds from their whipping (an action that demonstrates his repentance and his full reconciliation with them, with those whom he considered enemies) and they sit down at the table full of joy to celebrate. The passage does not say it, but we can assume that once the party was over, everyone returned to jail. Their reason for being there had been fulfilled. Then Paul demands his right to be freed from jail by the very magistrates, they do it but they expel them from the city. The church was born with a woman, a jailer and his family. They had received salvation, but they had contemplated the risks of being a new humanity. These were first discipleship lessons, but, none of them were discouraged and nobody thought it was too much.

## 2. INSTRUCTIONS FOR ADVANCED DISCIPLESHIP

Later on, Paul writes to his beloved faithful community. In what is one of his most beautiful expressions, he writes: "being confident of this, that he who began a good work in you will carry it on to completion until the day of Christ Jesus" (Phil 1:6). Discipleship is following Jesus in everyday life and the "graduation" will be the day of our encounter with the Lord and Master. In the meanwhile, the pastor prays for them day after day: "that your love may abound more and more in knowledge and depth of insight, so that you may be able to discern what is best and may be pure and blameless for the day of Christ, filled with the fruit of righteousness that comes through Jesus Christ" (Phil 1:9–11). May they be the living and concrete proof of the new creation!

The disciples' style of behaviour elicits different responses. Some are convinced that Christ has come to reconcile us with God, with our neighbours, with ourselves and even with nature. Thus, they willingly surrender their lives to the Lord and join the family of faith. The majority, however, respond with indifference, while others with opposition and even with violence.

Taking as example our experience, one day Christ sought to pitch his tent (John 1:1) in one of the most dangerous neighborhoods of Ciudad Cuauhtémoc (México), and many children began to arrive. They came with their laughter, their games and their noise. For a while, one of our neighbours would leave anonymous notes full of rude phrases under our door. He was upset; instead of seeing an opportunity for the children coming from broken families and an unhealthy social environment of gangs and drug dealers and lots of alcohol, he only saw the annoyance of the noise and the trash in front of our house. He could not understand that Christ was pitching his tent in the middle of this neighbourhood to love, rescue and provide them different opportunities in life.

When my family and I moved into an apartment in the city of Mexico and the neighbours found out that we were Christians, they came to warn that we could not hold church meetings or sing praises. They, however, often had outrageous parties that lasted all night.

Pastor Lorenzo (Lencho) told us that once, some men came to the church asking for a payment to protect him, and that if he refused then they would attempt to assassinate him. "No, my friends," he replied, "we already have someone who protects us and would be very offended if we accepted your offer. My life is in his hands, not in yours, so be careful," he told them.

"I seized the opportunity," said Lencho, "to tell them that we were going to preach the gospel in a remote village known to be occupied by drug lords. We went, with much fear of the risks, but the people received us well and we planted a church." Now this town is the scene of constant battles between the army, the police and the drug dealers. However, the brethren take refuge in the power and love of Christ.

Tears welled up in the eyes of David Wiebe, a Mennonite missionary who does missions with an indigenous group from the mountains, when he told us: "Every time I go, I do not know if I'm going to come back. The dangers are immense. Not a day goes by without receiving threats warning you not to return. But how could we not go? When I arrive, there are already three hundred and up to five hundred indigenous people waiting for the worship service." By the way, every time I have asked David when I can go with him, he answers: "wait," "not yet," "keep waiting." It's just that, as members of the family of faith, we take care of and protect one another other.

Another companion in the faith that comes to mind is Gabriel Orea and his family, who are missionaries in China. "You Mexicans do not have the resources or the infrastructure or the experience necessary to send missionaries to the world," an Anglo-Saxon missionary once told him. And yet, the Oreas set off for China. They went lacking resources, facing constant threats of expulsion from the government and dealing with a terrible illness, but this did not prevent him from fully devoting himself to the mission. They went "not fearing the king's anger; he persevered because he saw him who is invisible" (Heb 11:27). Another community of believers has been birthed in China.

So why do we go? Why do we take such risks? Actually, whenever we think of an area of the city or a town, we do not even ask ourselves these questions. What we say is, "we feel a burden for this place" and then we organize ourselves and go. We go without thinking about the risks; such is the love of Christ.

### 3. THE PRIVILEGES OF DISCIPLESHIP.

As we saw in the passage above, those who have believed in Christ have become his disciples; they are being formed into the image of the Master and have been commended with the mission of announcing the kingdom of God to the world. As we are in formation, some of the disciples will struggle with envy and conflict. A disciple is always in movement, on the way, permanently on mission (Matt 28:19). As they move, disciples have the privilege of experiencing the meaning of life in its fullness: "For to me, to live is Christ and to die is gain" (Phil 1:21).

From the beginning, the Anabaptists spoke about the "baptism in blood." They welcomed new believers with joy, but they also warned them of the risks that were involved; the *Martyrs' Mirror* tells us many of those stories. Today, we know about missionaries and pastors faced with persecution, imprisonment and even execution in Asia, Africa and Latin America. Mennonite magazines and newsletters talk about all these, but, there is much more that must be said so that the body of believers can be aware of the ways in which the powers are being confronted and how our mission is being strengthened and revived.

Likewise, the apostle does not shy away from this exhortation: "Whatever happens, conduct yourselves" (I repeat: whoever says that he or she knows Christ, must follow him in life) "in a manner worthy of the gospel of Christ" (make no concessions, compromises or alliances with the powers) ". . . stand firm in the one Spirit" (together with others, since the mission is a common task for all believers), "striving together as one for the faith of the gospel" (this means fighting: exerting yourselves, working hard, making sacrificing together) "without being frightened in any way by those who oppose you" (the gospel of peace will not be well received by all; there will be always opposition). The text closes with "For it *has been* granted to you on behalf of Christ *not only to believe in him, but also to suffer for him . . .*" (Phil 1:27–30, emphasis mine).

For believers, their encounter with Jesus is a moment of celebration and great joy in their lives. The light has come: life starts making sense and is filled with purpose and meaning. "One thing I do know. I was blind but now I see" (John 9:25), but, together with such enlightenment, we are granted to suffer for him.

We suffer, as nobody will congratulate us for embracing a new life. We suffer marginalization, we are pushed out, doors are closed to us, we are disinherited, we lose opportunities, communication with us is blocked, and we are cut off from networks. Missionaries leave "country and kindred"; we go from place to place. Our children grow up far from grandparents, aunts and uncles, and cousins. We often cry for friends with whom to talk and share. That is also suffering.

> Peter addressed the same subject: "Dear friends, do not be surprised at the fiery ordeal that has come on you to test you, as though something strange were happening to you. But *rejoice inasmuch as you participate in the sufferings of Christ*, so that you may be overjoyed when his glory is revealed. *If you are insulted because of the name of Christ*, you are blessed, for the Spirit of glory and of God rests on you. If you suffer, it should not be as a murderer or thief or any other kind of criminal, or even as a meddler. However, if *you suffer as a Christian, do not be ashamed, but praise God that you bear that name*. (1 Pet 4:12–16, emphasis mine).

## 4. CALLED TO BE IDENTIFIED WITH JESUS.

Jesus of Nazareth, the Son of God, the Saviour, reconciler, forgiver, lover and peacemaker, suffered opposition, persecution and death.

His own family members did not believe in him and they considered him crazy. The people of his town, where he grew up, rejected him as well. Many times, they tried to kill him. He lived surrounded by intrigues. They tried to discredit him by linking him with Beelzebub, accusing them of being "a drunkard," a friend of sinners. The official religion called him blasphemous. They classified him as "just one more," a seditious saboteur of the ancient traditions, a miracle-working sorcerer. They wanted to distract him from his mission by making him king. The people who acclaimed him turned their backs on him. His friends abandoned him in the darkest hour. And he also was betrayed, imprisoned, falsely accused, tortured and nailed to the cross. The Prince of Peace suffered the most merciless and inhuman torture.

Jesus said, "From the days of John the Baptist until now the kingdom of heaven has suffered violence, and the violent take it by force" (Matt 11:12). John the Baptist's ministry announced the hope that would come with the arrival of the Messiah and, at the same time, denounced sin in all its forms. The powers that promote the culture of death and injustice reacted violently and killed the prophet. This has always been the case: physical and structural violence is used to supress God's kingdom project.

The kingdom is the new project of God for humanity and its standard is love. Love for God, neighbour, self and nature. The reconciliation comes through repentance, confession of sins and renunciation of those sins. It is also comes through lives of forgiveness, giving, sacrificial surrender, mercy and compassion. Reconciliation also involves renunciation of private property and the accumulation of goods; it entails an open dinner table, worshipping God and serving the neighbour. This reconciliation is seen in the adoption of a simple lifestyle that does not insult the poor or the rich, that turns the other cheek in response to violent neighbours, that builds peace. Reconciliation means getting involved in situations where we are not necessarily welcome in order to bring peace. It is loving over and over again, despite rejection and hatred. Finally, reconciliation involves putting away the nationalism, racism, classism and religiosity that misappropriate God. It is about surrendering our whole life to the Messiah Jesus, being cleansed of sins by his blood, and thus living forever grateful.

This is the good news against which the powers react with violence. Is there joy and happiness by taking the gospel to all possible places? Yes, there is. Is there risk and suffering along the way? Yes, there is that too.

That is why it is like a sower who scatters the seed in a field, but where the enemy himself came to sow the darnel in an attempt to spoil the wheat. It also looks like something as insignificant as the yeast, which at the beginning is a just small of dough, but when we leave it resting, it expands by itself to become tasty bread. It is also like the mustard seed, the most insignificant of all the seeds but that when it grows, it becomes a big tree where we can find refuge, comfort and peace (Matt 13).

We give ourselves to carrying out the mission and persist faithfully. We will never fully know what kind of soil it is in which we're planting. But God will always have people who recognize the pearl of great price, people who see it for the treasure it is and which give up everything to have it (Matt 13:44-45).

A poor and old woman used to come by our house asking for water and something to eat. One day she told me that she needed a door and windows for her house. She lives in a town fifty minutes from ours, so we decided to go visit her. She told us then, "Here you can come and have worship services for the Lord." That day we started to interact with her neighbours, and although we knocked on their doors, most of them did not open to us. Missionary work that is measured by how many "souls" we gain for God is not worth it. Jesus' command to go supports the opposite. A door has been opened, albeit that of a poor and old woman, but still a door. The growth of the mustard seed will be a miracle that the Holy Spirit produces. So, those who have ears to hear, listen.

## CONCLUSION

We who are followers of Jesus are the salt of the earth and the light of the world. Even if we have become a saltshaker tucked away in a corner of the cupboard, we are still salt. If we are a shy light hidden under the table, we are still light. We cannot avoid being what we are. But in order to give flavour, we must get out of the salt shaker, and in order to illuminate, we must feed the fire and go to a high place. Is there joy and happiness by taking the gospel to all possible places? Yes, there is. Is there risk and suffering along the way? Yes, there is that too.

Because his extreme illness, Gabriel, to whom I have previously referred, knows that he could die in a strange country, a country with different customs and language. He knows that his wife and daughters could face a critical situation; Gabriel has always known that there are many risks in obeying the calling to go. However, he and his family are Christians who, without hesitation, would say, "it seems good to the Holy Spirit and to us as well." They know that the only one who can put an end to their work in China is the same

Lord who called them, and in the meanwhile they continue to grow in love and passion for God's mission.

Is there suffering? Yes, there is, but they would assure us without any doubt that "the sufferings of this present time are not worth comparing with the glory about to be revealed to us" (Rom 8:18). "When he opened the fifth seal, I saw under the altar the souls of those who had been slaughtered for the word of God and for the testimony they had given; they cried out with a loud voice, "Sovereign Lord, holy and true, how long will it be before you judge and avenge our blood on the inhabitants of the earth?" They were each given a white robe and told to rest a little longer, until the number would be complete both of their fellow servants and of their brothers and sisters, who were soon to be killed as they themselves had been killed" (Rev 6:9–11).

## STUDY QUESTIONS

1. What are the needs in our area to which the mission must respond urgently? How can we respond comprehensively to them?
2. Five hundred years into our Mennonite-Anabaptist heritage and in an increasingly globalized world, what is our understanding of discipleship? How do we contextualize the teaching of Jesus in our own lives, our family and the church?
3. What is the centre of our call to mission today? Think about: is it a good opportunity to get out of the routine? Does it only mean the prestige that a mission agency has hired us? Alternatively, is there a great passion,

compassion and willingness to assume gladly all that it implies?

4. In our daily life, how do we identify ourselves with Jesus?

5. How do we support to the churches/missionaries that today are suffering persecution by violent systems and for their faithfulness to Jesus Christ?

# Chapter 7

# Text: our authority for faith, life and mission

## Mvwala C. Katshinga

> **TEXT**
> *We hold and share the Bible as our authority for faith, life and mission. The Holy Spirit within and among us is the primary interpreter of the Word.*

### INTRODUCTION

In African societies, the word of a traditional chief has historically had the force of law and had to be followed. The respect given to the chief's word (message), as well as to the messenger, served as a barometer of the authority that the chief had among the population within his or her territory of influence.

The word of our God, the King of kings, deserves an even higher degree of respect from God's chosen people, the church, even though over the generations this respect has not always been the forthcoming. God's word – the Holy Scripture – is the foundation of the faith, because it is directly identified with God. This is the meaning of John 14:23 that states, "*In the beginning was the Word, and the Word was with God, and the Word was God.*"

In the history of our (Anabaptist) faith, and specifically in the sixteenth century, the question of authority in matters of faith and life was a pressing one in the church in general, and among the reformers such as Martin Luther, Zwingli and other Anabaptists. During that period, as noted by Donald McKim[98], three factors led to controversy regarding authority in issues of faith and life in the church of the 16h century. These were the authority of the Pope, of the Holy Scriptures and of church tradition. These three "authorities" were equally valued.

Over time, the Lutheran Reformation, with its well-known principle of "*sola scriptura*" – or Scripture alone, played a role in returning the church to its biblical foundations. Unfortunately, as it turned out, Luther and others who had initially made much of the slogan, did not emphasize the principle in daily life and faith.

The "brethren" – our Anabaptist ancestors – were among the first, if not the first, to take the courageous step of restoring the supreme and unqualified authority of Scripture in matters of Christian faith and life. Their single-minded belief in following all Scripture and applying it to daily life with an unconditional obedience, was considered as radicalism and utopian idealism by their contemporaries.

Palmer Becker writes:

> Early Anabaptists, including Menno Simons, were disappointed with the incompleteness of the Reformation. They did not want to merely reform the church back to the structures set in motion by Constantine and the theology of Augustine. They wanted to **restore** the church to its original New Testament pattern and form. They believed that the church needed to be

---

[98] Donald McKim, *Theological Turning Points. Major Issues In Christian Thought* (Atlanta: John Knox Press, 1988).

an independent and alternate society in the world.[99]

Today, five hundred years later, many Christians share these beliefs. The Anabaptists were right, despite the persecution that they suffered at the hands of the civil and religious authorities. Those authorities mistakenly saw Anabaptists in the same light as other unruly heretics, whom they felt should be banished from the earth. For Anabaptists, if belief in God was a question of choice, then obeying God's Word was an obligation that followed from that belief.[100]

Having said that, we as the churches that have often been called "believers churches" have a heritage to nurture and share with respect to the authority of Scripture in matters of faith and life. History proves this, and our current context confirms it. From Grebel's time to our day, efforts have been made – despite many challenges – to assure that our journey toward eternity is illuminated by the light of Scripture.

## 1. THE SCRIPTURES IN ANABAPTIST/MENNONITE LIFE, YESTERDAY AND TODAY.

It could be said with respect to the Reformation history of the church in general that Anabaptism has been a positive consequence of the high importance accorded to Scriptures rather than human beings, tradition, habits and customs – in matters of faith, life and missionary zeal.

In the evolution of the Anabaptist movement from its beginning, three key moments reinforced the importance and weight of the Scriptures. These were the ministry of Conrad Grebel and his companions, the gathering at Schleitheim and

---

[99] Palmer Becker, "What is an Anabaptist Christian?," *Missio Dei* No 18 (Elkhart: Mennonite Mission Network, 2013).

[100] Nzash U. Lumeya, "Course on Introduction to Mission," Kinshasa, University Mission Center, 1999.

the elaboration of the Common Convictions by the Mennonite World Conference (MWC) (which I prefer to call the "Mennonite World Community").

## 1.1. GREBEL AND THE AUTHORITY OF SCRIPTURE

In referring to Grebel, we in fact think of all those in the sixteenth century, who were guided by the Holy Spirit as they insisted on believing, living out and obeying God in such a way that a reform-minded church remained faithful to the Holy Scriptures. It is important to remember that Anabaptism was born on 21 January 1525 at a Bible study and prayer meeting. Conrad Grebel and his colleagues were convinced that the Holy Scriptures were the sole authority for the resolution of problems on matters of faith, in opposition to those who mistakenly felt that influences other than Scripture should have a decisive role.

It was through a careful reading of the Scriptures, rather than listening to the theological arguments of Zwingli and other intellectuals of the time or being influenced by fear of reprisals of the political authorities, that Grebel and his friends rejected infant baptism and the involvement of the state in deciding matters of faith among Christians.

It was also through an unconditional obedience to God's Word that the first Anabaptists understood their missionary responsibility to preach the gospel to all creation, based on Jesus' words and the faith modelled by Christians of the earliest church. Conrad Grebel, George Blaurock, Félix Manz, Michael Sattler and others willingly risked their lives, following the example of Stephen (Acts 7). These Christians paid with their blood so that the Scriptures would retain their place and full authority in the church. As a result, we as Mennonites today still understand the Scriptures in this way in our churches.

Though they were sometimes seen as radicals, this group of Anabaptists Christians and those who followed, such as Menno Simons, put the Scriptures at the center of Christian life and action. They further oriented the church as a whole toward its current practice of congregational study of Scripture, adopting a community-based understanding of scriptural interpretation, as suggested by Acts 2:42–47.

In sum, these brothers (and unnamed sisters) wanted to identify with Christians of the early church, who understood that God, through Jesus Christ and by the power of the Holy Spirit, was with those who were obedient to God's Word. In such a community of saints (the church), the reading and sharing of God's Word, prayer, communion and unconditional discipleship were the primary characteristics.

Over time, as a variety of small groups of Anabaptists emerged, each with its own particularities, another key moment took place. The leaders of these small Anabaptist groups met at Schleitheim in Switzerland (1527) to clarify certain doctrinal matters. Primary among these matters was the place of Holy Scriptures.

### 1.2. SCRIPTURE AT THE SCHLEITHEIM ASSEMBLY

The *Brotherly Union* at Schleitheim was the setting for the first consensual document produced by the Anabaptists, two years after their formation. This document lays out the doctrinal principles to be followed in the practice of the faith. It contains seven key points, on baptism, the Lord's Supper, pastoral leadership, excommunication, separation from the world, non-violence and the taking of oaths.

The gathering at Schleitheim, Switzerland, in February 1527 was necessary because the various small groups of Anabaptists were not homogeneous. The document produced from this gathering, referred to as the "Brotherly Union of

Schleitheim," became known as the "Schleitheim Confession."

Regarding the fundamental motivation for this historic doctrinal gathering, note this extract of the English translation:

> But for you it is not so; for they who are Christ's have crucified their flesh with all its lusts and desires. You understand me well, and [know] the brothers whom we mean. Separate yourselves from them, for they are perverted. Pray the Lord that they may have knowledge unto repentance, and for us that we may have constancy to persevere along the path we have entered upon, unto the glory of God and of Christ his Son. Amen.[101]

While the authority of Scripture is not specifically addressed among the seven listed doctrinal points, the document is clearly rooted in the Word of God, and it applies in a foundational way the principle of *sola scriptura*. This is demonstrated by the fact that each point of doctrine is backed up by biblical references.

A new development with this document is that while initially only the issue of baptism was highlighted by the Anabaptists, here seven priority subjects were brought to the attention of Christians regarding the practice of their faith. In the context of persecution and dispersion, the gathering of

---

[101] Translation by John H. Yoder, based on a version of the text prepared by Heinold Fast for *Quellen zur Geschichte der Taufer in der Schweiz*, and published by Herald Press in 1977.

Schleitheim was one of true theological consolidation. It allowed Anabaptism to put forward clear arguments in response to their Protestant, Catholic and political detractors.

For this reason, Cornelius J. Dyck[102] suggests that the gathering at Schleitheim, the first of its kind, contributed to the survival of Anabaptism on two levels. First, it took place at a critical moment to distance Anabaptism from both the conformists and the extremists. Secondly, the doctrinal position elaborated in the declaration is simple, biblically based, comprehensive and understandable enough that any Christian could follow it and accept to suffer for its principles.

By means of this *Brotherly Union* firmly based on Scriptures, Anabaptism received a new breath of life and expanded – against the prevailing winds and tides – into many European countries. There, some of its supporters were known by the name "Mennonite," a title derived from the name of one of their leaders. Today these Anabaptists have multiplied to such an extent that it became important to create a common platform through the Mennonite World Conference.

### 1.3. THE HOLY SCRIPTURES WITHIN MENNONITE WORLD CONFERENCE

As we have noted, the expansion of Anabaptist-Mennonite faith has not been limited to Europe. It has also included the Americas, and today Mennonites are present on five continents. From the sixteenth to the twenty-first century and continuing with the creation of Mennonite World Conference (MWC), Christians from the Anabaptist tradition have always seen the Scriptures as their sole authority in matters of Christian faith and life. Mennonite World

---

[102] Cornelius J. Dyck, *An Introduction to Mennonite History,* (Pennsylvania: Herald Press, 1967).

Conference is not a structure belonging only to the Anabaptist founders of the sixteenth century, nor to their respective nationalities (Swiss, Dutch, German, etc.). Rather it is a global, multicultural church today made up of 1.4 million members from 107 conferences in 87 countries.[103]

As was the case at Schleitheim, as the Mennonite World Conference Anabaptist family became larger and increasingly heterogeneous, it became necessary to reaffirm and readjust its Christian doctrinal principles. While one can be proud to belong to a large spiritual family, it is important to maintain the equilibrium of such a family based in the biblical values and life principles of the community.

Happily for the Mennonite World Conference, the results of a study carried out in 2013 by the Institute for the Study of Global Anabaptism, involving 24 member conferences, confirmed among other things that the vast majority of those participating considered the Bible as the Word of God.[104] This study thus reaffirmed the foundational principle that all Anabaptist-Mennonite churches are committed to, namely the authority of Scriptures. It also reconfirms the validity of the seven Shared Convictions of the Anabaptists worldwide. These were adopted earlier, on 15 March 2006 by the General Council of Mennonite World Conference in Pasadena, California in the USA.

Among these seven Shared Convictions, the fourth one is essentially focused on the authority of the Scriptures. It is expressed in these terms:

---

[103] Karla Braun, "What's an Anabaptist," *Courier* 31 No. 2 (October 2016), 2.
[104] Elizabeth Miller, "A Unique Opportunity for Greater Unity," *Courier* 31 No. 2 (October 2016), 3–7.

> As a faith community, we accept the Bible
> as our authority for faith and life,
> interpreting it together under Holy Spirit
> guidance, in the light of Jesus Christ to
> discern God's will for our obedience.[105]

This conviction of MWC insists not only that the Scriptures have authority, but also that their interpretation is not the monopoly of a single person. Rather the Spirit of God speaks through the church, and it is the church that is the spokesperson for God, and the Holy Spirit the ultimate interpreter of Scriptures in the world.

That is why, in an MWC that is increasingly large and diverse, we agree with John Driver who counsels a spirituality consistent with "living together in the Spirit," nourished and shared by the community of faith. This vision thus reemphasizes a "community hermeneutic" or the collective interpretation of Scripture, rather than an interpretation imposed by a church hierarchy. The Bible does not recognize completely individualized spiritualities, a concept that is in any case destined for extinction.[106]

Through this overview of past and present, it is clear that Anabaptist Christians believe, live out and share their faith conforming to the Word of God, the Holy Scriptures. They recognize that they are in the world without being of the world.

It can be said with confidence that the Anabaptist-Mennonite churches understand and share the Bible as their sole authority in matters of faith, life and the evangelization

---

[105] John Driver, *Life Together in The Spirit. A Radical Spirituality for The Twentieth-First Century* (Walden: Plough Publishing House, 2015).
[106] Cf. Janet Plenert, "The Witness of Unity," *Courier* 29 No. 5 (October 2014), 9–10.

of the world. Thanks to the power of the Holy Spirit, they interpret Scripture together, in community, as God speaks through the church rather than individuals.

## 2. ISSUES FOR BIBLICAL MISSION IN A GLOBALIZED WORLD

Anabaptists are Christians who have from the beginning been strongly mission-oriented. They believe in God's love, and that it is to be shared with others. Their understanding of mission is Bible-centred and holistic, because it is based on God's word rather than on the philosophy of a human being or a structure. Jesus Christ is the missionary model to be followed. (Matt 28:16–20; John 17:18, 20).

This mission orientation is holistic because it focuses on all aspects of human life: the soul, the spirit and the body. The gospel must demonstrate the conviction that human beings are created in God's image regardless of culture or geography (Gen 2:27; Matt 18:1), thus mission is carried out by Anabaptist-Mennonite organizations focusing on a variety of services such as health, education, peace and reconciliation, etc.

But already the Anabaptist community is increasingly confronted with challenges of globalization and diversity This requires that the community be firmly based on Scriptures to assure that its mandate is biblically based. Our governments, our cultures, our educational systems and our contemporary visions of the world suggest alternative perspectives on faith and life that are contrary to the Holy Scriptures and our Christian history.

To take up the missionary challenges of our time, Anabaptists must work hard to preserve their Anabaptist heritage, promoting an understanding of leadership that is transformational, carefully managing the resources of the global community.

## 2.1. *THE PRESERVATION OF THE ANABAPTIST HERITAGE*

The faith, life and mission commitment of the first Anabaptists represent a precious legacy that our generation must not cast aside under the influence of a seductive and risky modern culture. The early Anabaptist brothers and sisters remained true to Scripture despite diverse and constraining ideological pressures. Because of a Bible-centred faith, their involvement in the world was consistently holistic and focused on mission. Faith in Christ maintains its value when it is communicated to others, particularly others who are not of the same culture, race, social class, intellect, etc. And this communication can be done through prayer, giving or through service – in the flesh.

This Anabaptist mission praxis preceded the modern missionary era initiated by the works of William Carey and focused further by thinkers like Donald McGavran, Peter Wagner, Ralph Winter, etc. Even if the terminology has changed, the practice and understanding of mission by Anabaptists today remains very original.

But how can the Anabaptist missionary heritage be maintained when the Anabaptist churches of today are so open to the incursions of global conformity? How can today's Anabaptist Christians be considered worthy heirs of the Anabaptist legacy when they trample underfoot what they have gained by adopting certain falsehoods that have been legitimized by governmental and church institutions? How can we preserve the heritage of spiritual unity and sense of community when Anabaptist women are considered as not being blessed by the Holy Spirit to the same extent as men for the exercise of the missionary mandate?

These are some of the challenging questions that the Anabaptist community of faith faces and will continue to face during this critical period of globalization. Today's Anabaptist churches have a heavy responsibility to preserve the precious missionary legacy which was purchased by Jesus' blood and by the biblically-based faith of our spiritual ancestors. For without mission, there is no church; and without missionary practice there is no faith.

## 2.2. PROMOTING TRANSFORMATIONAL LEADERSHIP

A church with a missionary calling such as the global Anabaptist community needs to develop leadership by transformed men and women who will in turn transform others. It is the leadership model of Jesus, that of servant-leadership rather than master-leadership, that is needed. This kind of leadership pays attention to everyone, not just a few; it attracts rather than repels, and consoles rather than bringing sadness.

Thus, the Anabaptist Christians of the world must resist all temptations of cultural, racial, intellectual, material or financial domination. When the church grows and integrates new gifts, abilities, methodologies and needs, the leadership must pay attention to the guidance of the Holy Spirit regarding the message of the Scriptures. All conflicts around social class, race, country of origin, position and personal prestige must give way to a concern for the preservation of church unity. As Ephesians 4 reminds us, the diversity of gifts in the church is a source of wealth as long as each person finds her or his place according to the Lord's call. The field is large, and there are many workers filling our local congregations around the world who are there for the glory of the saints of our global community (Rev 7:8–9).

To this end, ongoing, informal Anabaptist formation must always be a priority in order to help the leaders and members of our church strengthen our rich missionary heritage. Our diversity should not compromise our values of faith and life and Christian mission.

If the challenges of leadership are resolved, good management – or the sharing of the resources available through our churches around the world – can be done without competition or discord (Acts 6:2–7).

## 2.3. THE MANAGEMENT OF RESOURCES AND GIFTS OF THE GLOBAL CHURCH

Another challenge of life, faith and missionary engagement when a church grows is that of distributing the resources of the community. This aspect can have a positive or a negative influence on the church in mission.

In this regard, Acts 2:40–47 can be read together with Acts 6:1. In effect, if the first text shows how unity is built and used, the second text underlines the danger that can undermine the church if the management of resources is not done properly. If the social needs of certain groups in the church are not met, and if gifts are inadequately shared, the unity of the church can be disrupted. How could these sisters and brothers, so recently filled with the Holy Spirit, act in this way? The global Anabaptist community – the church in mission – must not spare any effort to correct imbalances when there is a need for the same.

### CONCLUSION

Finally, we can say that the path of our faith community since 21 January 1525 until today is one of a people in mission with God. Our mandate is based on the Scriptures, in the light of the work of Jesus Christ and the ministries of the apostles, with the power of the Holy Spirit. Mission is our heritage, and the Bible remains our guide in all circumstances.

## STUDY QUESTIONS

1. What are the Christian practices that Anabaptist Mennonites have always maintained through seeing the Bible as their sole authority in matters of faith, life, and commitment to mission? (Acts 2:41–47)

2. What are the current or modern concerns that require Christian vigilance on the part of the Anabaptist-Mennonite churches, in order to preserve their inheritance in the area of faith, life and mission commitment? (John 14:15–21)

3. How can the gifts of each Anabaptist congregation be a blessing to the global Mennonite family? (Eph 4:1–16).

# Chapter 8

# Worship and mission

Janie Blough and James R. Krabill.

> **WORSHIP**
> We gather regularly to worship, celebrate the
> Lord's Supper and hear and respond to the
> Word of God in mutual accountability.
> Our worship is an integral part of equipping us
> to participate in God's mission.

## INTRODUCTION: INSEPARABLE PARTS OF GOD'S RECONCILING PROJECT

One of the identifying signs of the church is reflected in life together as a reconciled and unified body of worshipers gathered around and sent forth by the Reconciler, God incarnate in Jesus Christ.[107] Worship and mission are, in the Christian view, integrally related and inseparable components in God's project of the redemption of all creation.

This is the gospel shared both *within* and *without*. "The key to mission is always worship. You can only be reflecting the love of God into the world if you are worshipping the true God who creates the world out of overflowing self-giving love. The more you look at that God and celebrate that love, the more you have to be reflecting that overflowing self-giving love into the world."[108]

---

[107] See Rom 5:10–11; 2 Cor 5:18–19, Eph 2:14–16; and Col 1:19–22.
[108] N. T. Wright, "Mere Mission", Interview in *Christianity Today*, January 2007, 41.

Worship encompasses and joins together redemption in and through Christ in the power of the Holy Spirit. Facets of this worship include peace and justice, the enactment of reconciliation with God and one another (confession, forgiveness, baptism and communion), unity in diversity, harmony and community.

The gospel in all its full-orbed richness must be announced (*kerygma*), lived (*koinonia*) and shown (*diakonia*). These three aspects are united in mission.[109] In this interplay, corporate worship – via the Holy Spirit – forms and transforms us to do God's purposes in our personal lives, in the church and in the world.

Mission forms this vision of worship and is at its center. "The church does not have a mission, but rather God's mission has a church – that is, the church serves God's mission."[110] Stated another way, "when our worship glorifies God, it does so by praising God for God's actions and attuning us to God's missional purposes. When God through our worship sanctifies us, God conforms us to God's missional character and empowers us to participate in the *missio Dei*."[111] In this inner and outer synthesis of worship and mission, God's project becomes an integrated whole in the understanding of the life and nature of the church.

---

[109] J. G. Davies, *Worship and Mission* (Eugene, OR: Wipf and Stock, 1966), 36.

[110] Ruth A. Myers, *Missional Worship, Worshipful Mission: Gathering as God's People Going Out in God's Name* (Grand Rapids: Wm. B. Eerdmans Publishing Co., 2014), 18.

[111] This expression, *missio Dei*, is a Latin term meaning "the mission of God" or "the sending of God." For the quote, see Alan Kreider and Eleanor Kreider, *Worship & Mission after Christendom* (Scottdale, PA and Waterloo, ON: Herald Press, 2011), 255.

"Worship sets us free from ourselves to be free for God and God's purposes in the world. The dangerous act of worshipping God in Jesus Christ necessarily draws us into the heart of God and sends us out to embody it, especially toward the poor, the forgotten and the oppressed. ..."[112] God's mission forms the church's worship. And worship in turn motivates and empowers the church for God's mission.

To effectively form and structure this "inside/outside" concept in worship practices, an analysis of how the gospel interacts with different cultures and contexts worldwide becomes essential.

### 1. FOUR WAYS WORSHIP AND CULTURE INTERACT

Insights from the Nairobi Statement on Worship and Culture[113] can facilitate this effort for member congregations of the global Anabaptist family. This statement highlights four fundamental principles that can relate dynamically to all settings worldwide in the understanding that worship is to be transcultural, contextual, countercultural, and cross-cultural.

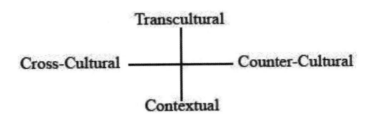

---

[112] Mark Labberton, *The Dangerous Act of Worship* (Downers Grove, IL: InterVarsity Press, 2007), 14.

[113] A document of study on worship of the department for Theology and Studies of the Lutheran World Federation.

- **Worship is transcultural.** The church is a worldwide family. Regardless of the culture, the basic gospel content remains the same for everyone everywhere. There is unity in our diversity because of the person and work of Jesus Christ who is the central driving force of our faith and the life of the church. We read the same Scripture and celebrate baptism and the Lord's Supper in an Anabaptist perspective. We believe the church is service oriented and missional inside and outside.

- **Worship is contextual.** The characteristics of the cultural context, specific questions, language, biblical insights, gestures, song and dress are valued and reflected in each church's worship patterns and ways of sharing the good news in the world. The Word needs to "become flesh" in each and every culture and context.

- **Worship is countercultural.** While each cultural context reflects the beauty of God's creation, it also has its sinful, selfish, greedy, war-mongering false gods that clash with and compromise gospel truths. Even as it affirms the positive aspects of culture, missional worship also announces gospel truths that denounce the multilayered dynamics of all idols in any given culture that do not conform to the values and purposes of God's reign. It further teaches believers how to resist them in ways that reflect Jesus' life and teachings and equips them to share with others God's desire to redeem and transform the world.

- **Worship is cross-cultural.** The celebration of Creation and Pentecost reminds us of the richness of unity in diversity. Our church life reflects this richness when we incorporate in our worship experiences songs, prayers and arts from faith communities in other cultures within our own neighbourhoods and from across the Anabaptist and broader Christian family worldwide. Such practices help to break down the cultural walls and ethnocentrism that often separate us. More importantly, they point us to the future that God is preparing when people of every tribe, tongue and nation will gather in worship around the throne of God and of the Lamb (Rev. 7:9).

## 2. FREE TO DEVELOP MISSIONAL WORSHIP FOR OUR CONTEXT.

If global Anabaptist communities open themselves to worship and mission practices that are rooted within the cultural contexts where God has planted them, we will witness a flourishing of creative expressions that are both faithful to the central message of God's reconciling work in Christ, while building on the rich cultural gifts God has showered upon them in their specific local and national settings. We see that freedom and liberty being given to God's people in increasing, incremental steps throughout the biblical story.

The Old Testament, as we know, is packed full of very specific laws and requirements on virtually all aspects of life. With regard to worship, there are worship spaces (the tabernacle and temple), worship times and feasts (Sabbath and Passover), worship furnishings (bowls, incense, and the ark of the covenant), worship officiants (priests and Levites), worship rituals (water cleansings and sacrifices), worship garments (*ephods*, breastplates and turbans), worship instruments (harps and cymbals), worship artists and composers (Bezalel, the sons of Asaph, and King David), and worship songs and liturgy (the Psalm collection and the public reading of the Law).

Mission itself was closely related to these worship patterns, for there was coming a day, proclaimed the prophet Micah, when peoples from all the surrounding nations would stream up to the Lord's house in Jerusalem, learn of God's ways, and sing Yahweh's songs on Mount Zion (4:1–2). "Mission accomplished" for the Hebrew people would happen in worship, in the Temple, and in Jerusalem – the veritable center of Yahweh's universe.

This all begins to change in the life, ministry and Great Commission of Jesus who sends his followers out of Jerusalem to the nations. "Mission accomplished" for the New Testament church would happen when groups of believers – as small in number as two or three – in every corner of the known world would gather in Jesus' name and worship God "in spirit and in truth" (John 4:24).

Now, there will necessarily be some "biblical constants" in this worship as we see modelled in early church practice – proclamation of God's Word, fellowship, prayer, praise, Christ-centredness, the Lord's Supper (Acts 2:42, 46-47) – as well as key "biblical principles" – God-focused, Christ-centred, Spirit-enabled, dialogical between worshippers and God, multivoiced, participatory and edifying both for individual worshippers and for the corporate body, equipping them for more effective participation in God's mission. [114]

But aside from these, the amazing freedom and flexibility that the New Testament grants to local communities of faith in developing their own forms and

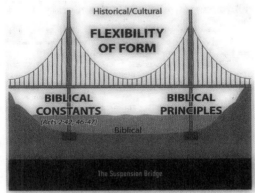

patterns of missional worship is nothing short of stunning. There appears to be little interest in the many objects and patterns of Old Testament worship, as if to encourage emerging congregations to find or create within their own widely-dispersed and varied settings the worship places, times, dress, furnishings and songs that build the local body of Christ in culturally appropriate yet faithful ways.

This dramatically transforms the missionary mandate of God's people, reminding them never to lock the gospel treasure of new life in Jesus Christ in any particular cultural

---

[114] These observations and the accompanying chart are adapted from the work of Ron Man in his chapter, "'The Bridge': Worship between Bible and Culture," in *Worship and Mission for the Global Church: An Ethnodoxology Handbook*, edited by James R. Krabill (Pasadena, CA: William Carey Library, 2013), 17–25.

pattern, but rather to encourage the creative work of the Holy Spirt in the lives of local believers in every time and place where the seeds of the good news are planted.

### 3. TWO CASE STUDIES –PAST AND PRESENT

"Almost every worship tradition we have is culturally shaped rather than biblically commanded. [. . .] There is a reason for the radical spirituality of worship in the New Testament. And the reason is this: the New Testament is a missionary document! The message found here is meant to be carried to every people on earth and incarnated in every culture in the world."[115]

It would be wonderful to begin documenting all of the many and diverse patterns of missional worship that are taking place in Anabaptist communities worldwide. What might we learn as we reflect more deeply and rejoice more fully in what God is doing through our extended family in almost one hundred countries around the globe?

Unfortunately, in this short chapter, we can do little more than highlight two brief case studies, one from our sixteenth century Anabaptist forerunners and another from a vibrant multicultural, urban Mennonite congregation in Paris, France.

### 3.1. *EARLY ANABAPTIST WORSHIP AND MISSION.*

From the very beginning, worship was a fundamental part of Anabaptist life. Its essence was rooted in the work and teachings of Jesus and in discipleship that resulted from a commitment to "observe all things" that Jesus had commanded (Matt 28:20).

---

[115] See John Piper in his chapter, "The Missional Impulse Toward Incarnational Worship in the New Testament," in *Worship and Mission for the Global Church: An Ethnodoxology Handbook*, edited by James R. Krabill (Pasadena, CA: William Carey Library, 2013), 101.

In reaction to the lavish pomp and pageantry practiced in the worship services of the state-supported churches of their day, Anabaptists wished to return to simpler patterns as observed by the early church. "When Anabaptists came together, they read the Bible, prayed, chose leaders, exhorted one another to be faithful in persecution, broke bread together, baptized, and debated with non-members in their midst."[116] In addition, "sacred hours, vessels, or places were not elevated above the rest of life because all of life was sacred."[117] "They felt no need to set aside a special time or place for this activity. Thus, they met at different times and places throughout the week when led by the Spirit."[118]

Anabaptists' deep passion for openly sharing their faith as commanded by Jesus in Matt 28:19–20 was the starting point for their understanding of the church to which all members were bound. The nature of their missional strategy was to be "in harmony with biblical teaching, effective when applied to mission situations, and relevant to the time in which it is used. There must be right goals pursued in a right place and at a right time with the right methods."[119]

Their mission fervour and the harsh persecution which soon followed also shaped their worship practices and prevented the emergence of a well-regulated congregational life. Much early Anabaptist worship took place at night, in the forest, on remote farms, in isolated mills or sheltered in huge

---

[116] In Alvin J. Beachy, "The Theology and Practice of Anabaptist Worship," *Mennonite Quarterly Review* 40 (July 1966), 166, citing John Howard Yoder.

[117] Paul M. Miller, "Worship among the Early Anabaptists," *Mennonite Quarterly Review* 30 (1956), 245.

[118] Edward L. Poling, "Worship Life in Sixteenth-Century Anabaptism," *Brethren Life and Thought* 37 (Spring 1992), 122.

[119] Hans Kasdorf, "Anabaptists and the Great Commission in the Reformation," *Direction* 4, no. 2 (April 1975), 303–318.

rock caves, far from authorities, and in hushed tones to avoid being detected.

Some worship gatherings were commissioning services for out-going missionaries in which candidates gave testimony to their calling and received prayer, counsel and encouragement for the dangers ahead. One remarkable twenty-five stanza hymn used in an early commissioning service recognizes the realistic possibility that those being sent forth might well "taste sword and fire" and never return:

> And if thou, Lord, desire
> And should it be thy will
> That we taste sword and fire
> By those who thus would kill
> Then comfort, pray, our loved ones
> And tell them, we've endured
> And we shall see them yonder—
> Eternally secured.[120]

### 3.2. THE CHÂTENAY MENNONITE CHURCH EXPERIENCE IN PARIS, FRANCE.

A more contemporary attempt to contextualize worship principles in an Anabaptist perspective can be found in the Châtenay Mennonite Church in the urban setting of Paris, France. There, an influx of people from many nations and cultures are seeking to give a positive, visible witness to the gospel message and the nature of Christ's church as a multicultural body through its worship and life together.

The Châtenay congregation began in the early 1950s with five people meeting in a bus parked in a working-class

---

[120] Hans Kasdorf, "The Anabaptist Approach to Mission, in *Anabaptism and Mission*," ed. Wilbert R. Shenk, (Scottdale, PA: Herald Press, 1984), 63.

suburb on the outskirts of Paris. At its origins, the congregation was almost exclusively white and middle class. Its members were primarily local Christians of various denominational backgrounds and rural ethnic Mennonites from eastern France who had moved to the city for jobs.

As ethnic migration from the Global South increased over the years and the population of the neighbourhood shifted, so too did the "face" of the worshipping community. With an influx of African, Haitian and other immigrants, the church has transitioned into a multiracial, multicultural, urban congregation. Such change means that the congregation must take seriously the gospel call to become a visibly unified and hospitable community amid great diversity in a highly secularized, post-Christian French context.

The congregation is small but thriving. The desire for biblically-based worship and unity in diversity are high priorities for its members. The very makeup of the congregation and the nature of the neighborhood are helping worshippers to become increasingly aware of the importance of becoming this visible sign of God's call to be a reconciled community where the walls of hostility caused by differences in culture, language, colour, gender or age are being broken down.

The missional challenge before the congregation is how to visibly affirm this biblical mandate in a common worship experience with believers of different Christian traditions and cultural backgrounds. How can one best learn that all have something to learn and understand from each other without forsaking beliefs, convictions and missional worship practices in an Anabaptist perspective?

There are several ways Châtenay works at this. The first is our common belief in God's Story recounted in Scripture. The biblical account of God's people is indispensable in defining who we are and is critical for an understanding of worship and mission, *inside* and *outside*. In this sense, missional worship and worshipful mission become one because The *story* told in worship informs and transforms believers into missional disciples who flow into God's missional project for the world. As Wilbert Shenk says: "The missionary disciple must be thoroughly immersed in the missionary message and ministry of Jesus."[121] Scripture readings used as in-between words to introduce the different elements of worship enrich this mission of transformation.

There are additional ways that the congregation works with intention at becoming a missional worshipping community. One is through the conscious choice of church leadership and preachers who mirror the congregation's heterogeneous group of believers. Another is a deliberate crossing of cultural frontiers in worship practices. Worship leaders from different cultural contexts enrich worship by giving a multicultural flavour to its content. Active participation of all members is encouraged, according to their gifts and style, including prepared and spontaneous prayer and song.

In the spirit of Col 3:16, Eph 5:18b–20, Rom 14:19 and 1 Cor 14:15–26, congregational singing constitutes an important element of worship. The musical plurality of the Châtenay congregation reflects the diversity of its members and gives broad expression of unity in a meaningful way. Effort is made to choose worship songs that reinforce the corporate and global nature of the church as the people of God

---

[121] Wilbert R. Shenk, "An Anabaptist View of Mission," in *Anabaptism and Mission*, eds. Wilbert R. Shenk and Peter P. Penner (Schwarzenfeld, Germany: Neufeld Verlag, 2007), 58.

and reflect the particular context of the congregation and its Anabaptist heritage.

In this important dimension of both worship and mission, attempts are made to teach important biblical and theological principles. The goal is to play a unifying role without surrendering the theological and historical marks of the congregation in an Anabaptist perspective, to edify the worshipping community and to expand its vision of the body of Christ worldwide.

Modest attempts to connect worship and mission in one congregation? Surely! Commitment to be faithful and join in God's project to reconcile all things in Christ? Indeed!

## STUDY QUESTIONS

1. What is your congregation's understanding of the vision of God's mission in the world? Describe how this vision impacts your worship practices, including congregational songs and other arts.
2. If believers are called to actively participate in this mission in their daily lives in the world, how do your congregation's worship practices inspire and equip believers for this work? If they do not, what changes would be necessary for this to be the case?
3. How can your local congregation create spaces and promote concrete forms of transcultural, contextual, countercultural, and cross-cultural worship? In what other ways are you discovering how to worship with the global faith family?

# Chapter 9

# The church dynamically engaging the powers

David W. Shenk

**UNITY and RESPECT**
*We promote the unity of all Christians as part of our witness, and we respect the people of other faith traditions as we share the hope that is within us.*

## INTRODUCTION

A century ago, my parents were pioneer North American Mennonite missionaries serving in East Africa in Tanzania (Tanganyika). They moved into the hamlet of Bumangi among the Zanaki people who had never heard the gospel before. Infant mortality was 80 percent. There was no literacy. The Great European war was raging. Petrol was mostly unavailable, and hence we rarely travelled. For us Shenk children, all of our boyhood friends were from Tanzania. Our friends taught us to hunt! We enjoyed being missionaries and often led our blind neighbour to church on Sunday mornings.

This essay especially looks at the challenges of pluralism within North American and African societies. We deliberately explore key mission challenges within very different societies: African and American. The challenges and differences provoke fresh understanding.

Respect for both North American and African societies was paramount. Mother often exclaimed, "How blessed we are to live among these wonderful African people." The emergence of a church at Bumangi was similar to church emergence in many communities across Africa. As first priority, my parents learned two languages. First was Swahili; that was the lingua franca of the traders. Then they learned Zanaki; that was the ethnic language of the tribal culture. My parents believed that community uplift and literacy went together. They also believed that the Word of God was an important step in becoming a disciple of Jesus. For that reason, my father, with an African colleague, translated the Gospel of Matthew into Zanaki. That was the first book ever translated into Zanaki.

## 1. The Disturbing Presence of Jesus in African Society

Bringing Jesus into the Zanaki worldview was a tremendous and revolutionary surprise. The Zanaki believed in a creator God who had gone away and would never return. Therefore, life after death was largely dependent on having as many children as possible. The gospel was a great surprise, because the gospel proclaims that God has come back and that God is love. Therefore, children did not provide salvation. Rather it is God in Christ who offers salvation for both for the living and for the ancestors who have died.

Very early on, it was evident that the disturbing presence of Jesus would bring conflict. One vicious conflict revolved around the ancestors. That conflict developed when the first Christian wedding happened, for the bride and groom were from different ethnic groups. That was taboo to marry across ethnic lines. Therefore, the elders of the clans cursed the couple so they would always be childless. The intention of the tribal elders was that the inter-clan marriage would be bereft of children. However, the couple was blessed with 13 children. The entire Zanaki nation was astonished.

The curse of childlessness was broken! Also transformed were other ethnic bondages of traditional Zanaki social practices. Literacy helped this process along by introducing new ideas into the society. Pride in language is one significant contribution. By spreading literacy, the missionaries were introducing pride in speaking and writing the mother-tongues of tribal society. Literacy unlocked enormous possibilities. When English and other international languages were introduced, the whole world became a potential learning laboratory. I grew up in that kind of culture. Both Zanaki and English thrived. North American missionaries enthusiastically participated in opening the door for literacy wherever they served.

However, the missionaries brought more than literacy. They also brought the knowledge of Jesus Christ. Wherever they went, North American missionaries brought the gospel. They planted churches. I am privileged! I was born just as the Mennonite North American global missions movement was getting under way. A movement to Christ such as Mennonite World Conference is evidence of the fruitfulness of the worldwide mission's movement of the last several centuries. When visiting a Maasai chief in Kenya, I asked him to state one special gift the gospel has brought to his people.

He replied, "Guests."

Then he elaborated, "Before the gospel came into my community, a stranger from another clan never visited me. Now guests from several communities come to drink tea with me under the branches of my acacia tree."

A global fellowship such as Mennonite World Conference is only one expression of transformations the gospel has brought. The intercultural fellowship of the gospel is transformative! The intercultural wedding at Bumangi was another evidence of the emerging church transforming ethnic boundaries in obedience to the welcoming mission of Jesus.

## 2. THE DISTURBING PRESENCE OF JESUS IN THE NORTH AMERICAN CHURCH

Mennonites have been greatly blessed as participants in the global missions movement. For an excellent history of the North American missions movement I recommend *Seeking Places of Peace*[122] This book describes North American Mennonites settling in North America. Then as they settled they turned outward in mission. Within a century of their arrival in North America, the Mennonites had established churches across North America and a few were seeking ways to extend internationally.

However, their first priority was their children; they evangelized their children quite fruitfully. A significant commitment to their children was the schools and universities that they began. Mennonite higher education has powerfully formed Mennonite self-identity and its mission.

Then in time, many were gripped by a vision for mission that reached out into regions beyond North America. The vision for mission often developed in most unexpected ways. There was Phoebe Yoder in Kansas who at twelve years of age promised the Lord that she would serve as a missionary in Africa. In 1943, she commenced the fulfillment of that calling by joining a Mennonite mission serving in East Africa. She served as a nurse and in leadership training.

In the meantime, in Pennsylvania two thousand miles east from Phoebe's Kansas home, twelve-year old John

---

[122] Royden Loewen and John A. Lapp (ed), *Seeking Places of Peace: A Global Mennonite History* (Good Books, 2012).

Mellinger asked his father why the Mennonites were slow to obey the Great Commission. Mellinger was troubled that Mennonites had not yet commissioned missionaries to take the gospel to all nations.

Although John never served in mission abroad, his questions led him into engagement in administration. His vision soon took North American Mennonite missionaries around the world. The calling to proclaim the gospel among all peoples led North Americans to sail from country to country, from village to countryside, from city to city to proclaim the gospel. Most often, these missionaries served with emerging local churches.

The witness to the gospel has often proceeded gently. For example, I consider the calling of another young person, Amanda Musselman, who walked through a blizzard in Lancaster County, Pennsylvania, USA, for a Bible study that would better equip her to serve in urban missions. Thereafter she and her colleague Mary Denlinger served in Chicago. Then Amanda moved to Philadelphia; thousands of urban children participated in the summer Bible schools offered by Amanda and the team working with her in the Philadelphia region.

Mennonite rural culture and American city culture created a remarkable synthesis. It is not surprising that Mennonites often became respected sociologists and anthropologists as well as biblical scholars. Wherever they went, Mennonites were known as people of the Word who were committed to Jesus Christ. Their witness has been Christ-centred and church centred. Mennonites overall bring into their mission a keen commitment to Jesus Christ in his fullness.

Missions in the cities were quite an adventure for North American Mennonite missionaries. The same is true of

Mennonites serving internationally. In 1934, the first team of missionaries from Lancaster, Pennsylvania, went by train to the New York City harbour to commission the first missionaries from the Lancaster area. Four hundred seventy-five went to New York City on that memorable day. The front page of *The New York Times* reported the event. At the stroke of mid night, the *SS Deutschland* weighed anchor with the first Mennonite missionaries who would serve in Africa (Tanzania/Tanganyika). Three missionaries set sail for East Africa that evening!

That was a beginning of Mennonite North American global and international missions. Today Mennonite missions proceed from everyone to everywhere. There are more than two million Mennonites living and ministering within at least 100 countries. A century ago, we would not have imagined such growth and vitality as we experience today within the mission of the global church.

### 3. A VISION OF THE WORLDWIDE CHURCH

The missionary theology of the first century's apostolic churches is well summarized in Rev 5. The main themes of a New Testament theology of mission are described in these 14 verses (Rev 5:1–14).

The chapter opens with God on his throne holding a book bound by seven seals. No one is worthy to break the seals. Surely the seven seals are a metaphor of the destiny of history. The destiny of history is held by the One who is worthy to open the seals. The One with that authority must be the authority who can bring to pass the just and good destiny for history.

The grand question is who is able to open the seals? The One worthy is the One who will bring history to its grand consummation. The consummation of history will be determined by the One who gives the true answer and the good news answer to the ultimate questions of human existence. The One who unlocks the grand plan must be the One who has authority and power to bring redemption to pass for all humanity and all creation. The One with authority must be the One who provides the right and true answer to the ultimate questions of existence. The One worthy to take the book is the One who is able to bring healing for the person and for our nations and communities. The inside of the book reveals our need for the miracle of grace and forgiveness.

There are fundamentally three of these ultimate questions: Why am I here? How can I be forgiven for my short coming? What is the meaning of death?

The self-appointed jobs of the religions and ideologies is to answer those three questions. The One who is worthy must bring hope into our world with its 50 million migrants and refugees. The One who is worthy must bring about a new creation. We need healing! We need a healer who restores and recreates our broken lives.

So, the grand search begins. Every religion and ideology enter the search. Messengers traverse the heavens; that is where the gods dwell. Other messengers go into the realms of the ancestors. Then there are other messengers who traverse the earth, into the realms of ideologies, such as Marxism. Alas, none of the messengers finds anyone worthy to take the book, because none are able to give good news and a true response to the ultimate questions.

For example, the Hindus proclaim that we are a tragic accident that should never have happened. Or examine the Buddhists who proclaim that there is no forgiveness. Or interview the Muslims who proclaim that there can be no such thing as confidence that our wrongful deeds are forgiven.

Science comes up short by announcing that human beings are only intelligent animals.

The apostle John to whom God is revealing the meaning of the book and its seals weeps at the pathos of it all. Not one of the world religions or ideologies is able to provide a true answer and a good news answer to these ultimate questions. For example, after searching the heavens and the earth the messengers announce that there is no assurance of the forgiveness of sin. None! John weeps huge tears. That weeping is experienced around the world.

The various gods and authorities present their credentials. Buddha is there recommending the great renunciation. Islam is there with its balance scales. The ancestors are there and the nature gods. None is capable to giving good news in regard to our destiny.

Then a great angel approaches John and proclaims! "John, dry your tears! The One worthy to open the seals has prevailed."

With enormous excitement John peers into heaven and he sees the Lion of Judah and the Root of David. He sees the one who carries king David's lineage of kingship. This Jesus whom John sees is not an afterthought in the mind of God. Indeed not! Rather he is the Lamb slain from the foundation of the world. He is the centre of God's grand plan to redeem and save us (Rev 13:8).

This means that the destiny of history is rooted in real history and real events. This is not a fairy tale. The One who is given the authority to open the seals is a real man. He comes from a real tribe with a real genealogy, Judah. He carries the real authority of a real king. When old man Jacob (Israel) was dying he called his twelve sons around him. He bequeathed each son a blessing. When he came to his fourth born, Judah, he proclaimed that from Judah a ruler would come to rule the nations. Thereafter the promise was made clearer in the prophetic promise that an eternal king would come from David's line. As the church responds to the call of God to be witnesses among all nations, we carry forward that witness recognizing that the One who has authority to open the seals is the One who has come to us through David's line and through the line of the Lion of Judah.

At the front of the church at Bumangi there was a Scripture verse inscribed by the first missionaries among the Zanaki people: "For God so loved the world that he gave his one and only Son that whoever believes in him should not perish but have everlasting life!" (John 3:16). That is the real event in real history that the missionaries proclaimed to the Zanaki people

However, as John peered into heaven it was a Lamb crucified and risen that he saw. Truly the One worthy is both king or lion, but at the soul of the Gospel, is Jesus Christ crucified and risen. Jesus the Lamb of God is able to break the seals that have bound the nations from becoming the communities of peace God intends.

The Lamb in God's plan is worthy because in his crucifixion and resurrection he has redeemed people from every tribe, and language, and people, and nation. That is why Jesus is given all authority; that is why he is given the book. In what happened in the cross and resurrection God redeemed people from around the world who serve in Christ's eternal kingdom (Rev 5:9–10).

In one of my visits to Bumangi the church was filled with five hundred people present for Sunday worship. The choirs sang special songs for the occasion, which was a visit of our family. Then the oldest believer in Zanaki land wended her way to the front of the throngs filling that church. She was locked tightly with arthritis. Nevertheless, as she danced and moved toward the front I saw her holding a tattered booklet as high as she could. She was singing exuberantly, "The book tells all about Jesus. He is the Saviour!"

She was holding high the Gospel of Matthew that my father and his Zanaki colleague had translated so many years ago! That morning in special ways Jesus joined us in the songs of praise.

### 4. A CHURCH FROM EVERY PEOPLE

We were singing of Jesus who is the Lamb of God who forms the church. The seven spirits go forth through all the world creating the church. These spirits are a metaphor of the Holy Spirit in all fullness calling forth the creation of the church (Rev 5:6–7). In these brief verses, we see the Trinity of God who sits on the throne, sends forth the Holy Spirit in fullness, and who redeems all who believe forming all believers into the people of God who shall serve the Lord in his kingdom forever.

All of creation joins in the choirs of joy as they participate in God's grand plan to restore and redeem people who will serve in Christ's kingdom forever. The whole universe joins in the songs of praise,

"You are worthy to take the scroll and to open its seven seals, because you were slain and with your blood you purchase for God persons from every tribe and language and people and nation. You have made them to be a kingdom and priests to serve our God and they will reign on the earth!" (Rev 5:10).

How can this happen? Through the mission of the church (Rev 6:1–2).

In chapter six, we see God sending a white horse with a message. The white horse is victorious. Bible scholars differ in regard to the meaning of the white horse. However, the early church generally agreed that the white horse and the rider is the church bringing the gospel. In that case, Matt 24:14 is the meaning of the white horse. It is a metaphor of the church taking the gospel from people to people.

That was the sermon text when our church at Bumangi sent its first missionary to a nearby clan. The preacher proclaimed that our church was sending forth the gospel to peoples who had never heard of Jesus. In Revelation, likewise, we see the church sending forth missionaries to people who did not know the gospel. There are many signs of the kingdom of God coming, such as wars and famines. However, Jesus proclaimed the most important sign in regard to the coming of the kingdom of God is the sending of the gospel to the nations.

Jesus declared, "And this gospel of the kingdom will be preached in the whole world as a testimony to all nations and then the end will come!" (Matt 24:14). That conviction encouraged the passion for mission that formed the young Mennonite churches that formed me within East Africa when I was a teenage missionary kid. I was immensely impressed that in sending missionaries from clan to clan we were participating with Jesus in the grand plan to proclaim the gospel to every people.

However, the context for mission is often terribly murky. A short review of the context for mission as described in Rev 6 is an example of the tragic contexts wherein mission so often happens. The metaphor of horses depicting our circumstances continues throughout chapter six.

The fiery red horse is the annihilation of peace in a violent world.

The black horse pummels the earth with famine that happens amid enormous wealth and luxury.

The grey horse is a stallion who brings death to a quarter of humankind.

Then there is the horse representing suffering and martyrdom.

Another horse depicts natural calamity

These horses are metaphorical descriptions of history. They are expressions of our tragic circumstances. I view these horses as descriptive metaphors of the ways of the nations as they live in disobedience to God. For example, we should not blame God for the wars; we sinful humans have created the wars. Yet within the wars, we see Christ bring healing and hope.

This morning, the news described thousands of refugees leaving Lebanon for Syria where they have nowhere to go. It is in the midst of such tragedy that the white horse (the church) is called to take Jesus our healer. Humanity weeps. There seems nowhere to turn. Yet in the midst of it all, we meet the church again and again ministering grace and healing.

I will restate the metaphors presented in the horses of Rev 6. This is how I see the horses; be free to develop your own understandings. First, the white horse with a rider is the church taking the gospel into the challenges and tragedies of history. Second, the other horses are the calamities that our sins bring upon us. Who is worthy and able to bring reconciliation in our homes, our lives, our communities, our histories. No one is found. It is in that context that God presents Jesus with the book. He is worthy. He is able. Only Jesus can bring about a new creation. Jesus brings forgiveness and reconciliation. Only Jesus can create the church, a community of forgiven sinners, a people who shall serve God in his kingdom eternally.

## CONCLUSION: A MESSAGE FROM EGYPT.

For the last fifteen years, my wife and I have invested especially in engagement with Muslims with a special focus on peacemaking. That is the reason not so long ago I was welcomed into the offices of the Grand Mufti of Egypt.

I explained that Jesus is the reconciler. I shared with the Grand Mufti how significant the crucifixion and resurrection of Jesus is in authentic peacemaking. I explained that Jesus breaks the cycle of violence and in his mercy, he offers us the gift of forgiving grace. We talked for about half an hour.

Then he invited me to come another time to continue the conversation, perhaps within a public forum. I was grateful and surprised by the invitation. The reader might be aware that Muslims generally deny the crucifixion of Jesus. Muslims believe that the cross suggests that God is bereft of power and authority. They believe that an almighty God cannot permit the Messiah to be crucified.

As I was leaving the cleric stopped me at the door while embracing me warmly. Then he said, "Tell the Christians in America to follow Jesus. When Christians follow Jesus they transform their society for good."

## *STUDY QUESTIONS*

1. In Rev 5, why does the apostle John and, in fact, all creation weep?
2. Why does the weeping turn to praise in Rev 5?
3. According to Rev 5, why is the church so important in God's plan?
4. Discuss this statement: Only Jesus gives a good news answer to the ultimate questions about the meaning of life.

# Chapter 10

# The fulfilment of our mission

César García

**FULFILLMENT**
*We eagerly await Christ's return and anticipate the final fulfillment of God's kingdom when people of every tribe, tongue and nation gather in worship around the throne of God and of the Lamb.*

## INTRODUCTION

The first time I saw a horror movie was one evening at a church. I was around eight years old when my mother took me to the premiere of a Christian film about the book of Revelation. That night I could hardly sleep. . . I dreamed that Christ had come for his church and that I had stayed behind to suffer what would be the great tribulation.

There are different ways of looking at the book of Revelation. Some of them, quite terrifying, fill people with fear. Some preachers use this book as some sort of crystal ball to discover the future and explain the events regarding the end of humanity. Countless films and books have fed on such ways of understanding this type of literature.

"Blessed is the one who reads aloud the words of this prophecy and blessed are those who hear it and take to heart what is written in it, because the time is near" we read in the first verses of Revelation 1:3. However, many modern approaches like the ones just mentioned end up removing the gladness promised to the readers of this text. How can we act on what is written there if it only has to do with forebodings of a distant future? Where can we find joy in the prophetic message if some interpretations present them so threateningly?

Part of the answer to these questions has to do with the way we approach the book of Revelation. As it is specified in the statement of the Mission Commission of Mennonite World Conference, presented in this text, as Anabaptists, we eagerly anticipate the return of Christ and the final fulfilment of the kingdom of God. With the phrase "we anticipate," we are not referring to a passive wait, but rather to a type of waiting in which that which we are expecting is reflected in our daily life and in concrete ways. In other words, as the Catholic theologian Rafael Gutiérrez affirms, human beings are not asked to enjoy the fulfilment of the kingdom of God in the future only, but rather we are invited to be a sign of the kingdom here and now, just as Jesus was.[123]

To be a sign or foretaste of the kingdom of God here and now is what brings joy as we discover God's will in the book of Revelation. It is in this sense that we affirm the fulfilment of our mission today as well as in the new creation. But, before going into more detail about what the fulfilment of our mission is, we must define here what we understand as *mission*.

By the term "mission" in this chapter, I refer to *everything* that the church *is* and *does* bearing witness to Jesus Christ in her ministry of reconciliation. Let me expand this definition a bit more:

---

[123] Rafael Gutiérrez Cuervo, *Cristología Y Moral: El Seguimiento De Jesucristo Como Compromiso Con La Justicia* (Bogotá: Pontificia Universidad Javeriana. Facultad de Teología, 2004), 92.

*Everything that the church is and does*

- The church *is* in herself a foretaste of the kingdom of God.

- The church does not have a message. She herself is the message.

- The church as a message implies her very presence. Any mission that is not communal and interdependent is weak.

- The presence of the church brings the announcement of the gospel of Jesus Christ through words and deeds, thus promoting reconciliation.

- The church's action in its testimonial work includes everything it does: worship, pastoral care, teaching, evangelism, service, peacebuilding and health ministries, among other things. What the church does or does not do, and how it does it, is part of its message.

*bearing witness to Jesus Christ*

- The message that the community shares through its words and deeds is delivered following the path of a witness, affirming their experience and testimonial knowledge. This implies an approach that is not imperialist (as if they were the master and keeper of the absolute truth), and it is not delivered from positions of human power. Rather, it is sharing "from below," with steadfast humility, our particular experience of faith.

- As the message is about Jesus Christ, it must be communicated from a position of vulnerability and service, just as Jesus himself did. This requires sacrificial surrender and a cruciform lifestyle that practices ministerial strategies consistent with the life and work of Christ.

- Taking into account the divine incarnation and the Christ's identification with discriminated persons, bearing witness to Jesus requires a serious contextualization of the message and an intentional identification with those excluded, ignored or victimized by society.

*in her ministry of reconciliation*

- The ministry of reconciliation has been entrusted to the church. This implies that the new life in community is, thanks to the Spirit, what makes it possible to experience reconciliation with God and among humans.

- The ministry of reconciliation seeks not only the salvation of the soul in the distant future, but the re-establishment of a full relationship with the Spirit of God and a life of just relationships which allow us to enjoy the peace which the same Spirit makes possible in the new creation.

When the mission is carried out across cultural barriers, then we speak of a transcultural or intercultural mission. This type of mission requires a level of training and preparation that facilitates the sharing among different cultures. Basic knowledge of anthropology and ethnology are very useful for this type of mission. It is important to clarify that this level of specialization does not ignore the aspects of the mission that I mentioned earlier; it rather seeks to apply them in new cultural contexts. For example, since the mission is communal and interdependent, the transcultural mission will seek to send micro communities that make present the life of the church and its work in a new cultural context.

Having defined here what we understand by mission, let us analyse how the fulfilment of this mission is Christ-centred, communal, multicultural and hopeful.

## 1. THE FULFILMENT OF OUR MISSION IS CHRIST CENTRED

The mission of God finds its reason for being and its ultimate goal in the person of Jesus. While the Gospel of John affirms that everything that exists was created through Jesus (John 1:1–5.), in the Pauline vision everything came to be *in* Jesus and has been reconciled *for* Jesus (Col 1:15–20). A similar idea is recorded in Rev 5:13–14 where everything created worships the One who has overcome.

But this overcomer in whom everything exists, the centre of our mission: who is he and what is he like? The same chapter 5 of Revelation, v. 2, gives us the answer when it states that only the Lion of the tribe of Judah, the descendant of King David, is worthy to open the scrolls. This affirmation occurs in the context of a great multitude of every tribe, language and nation. It is in this context that the Lion, the victor, the King, arrives . . . but he does so as a Lamb, a Lamb that has been sacrificed.

The book of Revelation constantly leads us to the image of Christ as a centre of worship. When we share our experiences of following Jesus in a context of intercultural diversity, we clearly see who and what God is like. It is in the midst of the worship of the multicultural community that we discover that Jesus defies our human standards of glory, authority, leadership and power.

According to Mennonite theologian John Driver, in the New Testament, the gospel of salvation comes to us from a position of socioeconomic and political weakness rather than from a position of economic affluence and human power.[124] The person of Jesus helps us understand that God defines his leadership as committed service and surrender. In the book of Revelation, the Lamb's authority derives from his sacrificial love for us, from the way in which he identifies with our pain and suffering.

This implies that our mission, if it has Jesus as its centre, must be framed by the form and content of Christ's message. As mentioned above, if the church intends to reflect Jesus, she needs to be incarnated in the community that surrounds it, identify with those it seeks to serve and act from a position of self-sacrificing dedication. Identifying with structures of human power and exerting pressure in an authoritarian or vertical way ends up obscuring the message of Christ.

The mission of God is then fulfilled in our lives when we act as a multicultural, global community, with Jesus as the centre of our work, following his example and living according to that reality. In this manner we enjoy a foretaste of the kingdom that is already among us, yet that is still to come.

---

[124] John Driver, "Messianic Evangelization" In Wilbert R. Shenk, *The Transfiguration of Mission: Biblical, Theological & Historical Foundations, Missionary Studies* (Scottdale, Pa.: Herald Press, 1993), 200.

## 2. THE FULFILMENT OF OUR MISSION IS COMMUNAL

According to 2 Corinthians 5:17-19 if anyone is in Christ, there is a new creation. It is in this sense that Driver reminds us: "The church not only proclaims the Kingdom of God, but it also is the community of the Kingdom, an anticipation (modest but authentic) of the Kingdom."[125] In the church the new creation, the eschaton, has already begun. "Wherever the Spirit of Christ, which as the eschatological gift anticipates God's new creation in history, is present in its *ecclesially constitutive* activity, there is the church,"[126] affirms the Anglican theologian Miroslav Volf.

As a new creation the church is called to live – here and now – in a new paradigm of life, this is, according to God's will for the world as it was evidenced in Jesus' words and life. This new life implies a radical rupture with secular values that glorifies egocentrism, classism, sexism and any other kind of discrimination and separation. The church is an anticipation of the kingdom of God in which "there is no longer Jew or Greek, there is no longer slave or free, there is no longer male and female; for all of you are one in Christ Jesus" (Gal 3:28).

"We look forward to the day when our coming, common hope – the Lord Jesus – will make us one. We must live today in view of that day . . ."[127] say evangelical theologians Brad Harper and Paul Metzger. We do not need to wait until the second coming of Christ to experience

---

[125] John Driver, *Contra Corriente: Ensayo Sobre Eclesiología Radical*, 3. ed., Colección Comunidad En Compromiso (Santafé de Bogotá, Colombia: CLARA, 1998), xv.

[126] Miroslav Volf, *After Our Likeness: The Church as the Image of the Trinity*, Sacra Doctrina (Grand Rapids, Mich.: William B. Eerdmans, 1998), 129.

[127] Brad Harper and Paul Louis Metzger, *Exploring Ecclesiology: An Evangelical and Ecumenical Introduction* (Grand Rapids, Mich.: Brazos Press, 2009), 35.

communion and unity. Furthermore, we are called to live as new creation in order to serve in the ministry of reconciliation. This ministry requires a completely new way of thinking, being and acting. It requires the mind of Christ that responds with love instead of retaliation in the midst of injustice and violence. The ministry of reconciliation requires a community that lives now in light of what will be. Otherwise, continue Harper and Metzger, "we will continue sending a very clear message to the surrounding, cynical world that our God's gospel is powerless to break down divisions among his people."[128]

Living the ministry of reconciliation does not mean putting aside our beliefs. According to Anglicans Phil Groves and Angharad Parry Jones, it means something far more threatening: "It means recognizing that the person you believe to be completely wrong on some issue of significance is on a journey with Christ and with you. It means trusting God together and not seeking to overwhelm the person with the force of your argument. It does mean being open to change, but to a change of heart and a desire to understand more fully your own walk with Christ."[129]

What can unite people or communities with different beliefs or backgrounds? Since the times of the Tower of Babel, many methods have been tried. Having a *common vision* that invites us to work toward the same purpose was the method attempted in that biblical story; and as it is well known, this attempt to reach unity failed.

Having a common narrative is another strategy that has been proposed to create unity. A unified history that describes

---

[128] Ibid. 281.

[129] Phil Groves and Angharad Parry Jones, *Living Reconciliation* (London: Society for Promoting Christian Knowledge, 2014), 32–33.

a common and inspiring origin can serve as a cohesive element. However, finding a stimulating narrative that involves people with different beliefs or diverse cultures is very difficult.

Another proven alternative in politics and religion for the sake of unity is to suppress all differences and promote the existence of a unique way of seeing life in order to destroy diversity. History shows us very clearly the failure that this alternative represents.

An option that is sometimes preached in ecclesial environments is the definition of a list of beliefs that must be held by a group of people to clearly determine who belongs or who is outside that group. Unfortunately, creeds and confessions of faith have sometimes been used in this regard.

What is it that makes it possible to live the ministry of reconciliation? It is not the text of our shared convictions at the Mennonite World Conference. This statement emerged in recent years as an expression of what is our experience of following Jesus in every context. The MWC member churches walked in unity without the existence of such text for more than seventy-five years. Nor is it a common story. Although as Anabaptist churches we identify with the Radical Reformation of the sixteenth century, it is clear that the complexity of the origins of our faith is as amazing as our current diversity.

According to the Scriptures there is only one possible explanation. The unity of our global community has not been the product of human efforts nor is it something that we manufacture. It is a gift from God that we can enjoy today through the work of the Holy Spirit in our midst. True communion is made possible not by laws and institutional formalisms, but by the work of Christ on the cross. That was where God created a new people composed of many cultures, races, tribes and languages. Today, it is only possible to sit at the same communion table and appreciate the beauty of our diversity if we do it around the Lamb of God who is the centre of our faith and who is the foundation of that unity.

Our societies need to see a different alternative to violence and resentment. People need to see palpable examples of reconciliation, love and forgiveness. The nations of the world need to see communities where nationalisms are overcome, where love is the mark of relations, forgiveness is a regular practice, and reconciliation is a reality that shows the kind of God that we believe in. Only these kinds of communities will have the right to be heard in contexts that are looking for new paradigms of peace and justice. In the words of Catholic theologian Gerhard Lohfink, "The real being of Christ can be bright only if the church makes visible the messianic alternative and the new eschatological creation that happens from Christ."[130]

### 3. THE FULFILLMENT OF OUR MISSION IS MULTICULTURAL

According to British mission historian Andrew F. Walls, "The very height of Christ's full stature is reached only by the coming together of the different cultural entities into the body of Christ. Only 'together,' not on our own, can we reach his full stature."[131] This is because the *whole* church is needed to know the *whole* truth.[132] The invitation then, which

---

[130] Gerhard Lohfink, *La Iglesia Que Jesús Quería: Dimensión Comunitaria De La Fe Cristiana,* 4a. ed. (Bilbao: Desclée de Brouwer, 1986), 191–92.

[131] Andrew F. Walls, *The Cross–Cultural Process in Christian History: Studies in the Transmission and Appropriation of Faith* (Maryknoll, N.Y.: Orbis Books, 2002), 77.

[132] Groves and Jones, xx.

Catholic theologian Emmanuel Katongole calls the Ephesian moment,[133] is to understand *mission* as God's activity of uniting various social fragments – as parts of the same body – in order to discover what Paul describes as "the measure of the fullness of Christ"(Eph 4:13).

In the book of Ephesians, the "aha" moment of reaching the full stature of Christ happens when we are sitting at the same table eating with people from different cultures. In this multicultural environment, we see the complete image of Jesus. There is not a single culture that sees the whole picture. When a part of the body is not present, the picture is incomplete. In the same way, the book of Revelation calls us to live right now according to that vision, a vision where there are no more nationalisms and the only foundation is Christ.

When I look at Scripture, I find at least three reasons why we need a global, multicultural and very diverse community:

First, *Jesus*. There are four Gospels that speak about Jesus. Each of them reflects the experience of its author with Jesus Christ. These theological writings do not show Jesus in exactly the same way. There is a lot of diversity among them. Why we do not have just one Gospel? Why do we need four different points of view that give different understandings about Jesus? From its very beginning, the church saw this diversity as something crucial, something that could help us to understand who Jesus is. The early church did not try to harmonize the four Gospels in order to give us a unique and uniform account about Jesus. We need diversity in order to know Jesus better.

---

[133] Emmanuel Katongole, "Mission and the Ephesian Moment of World Christianity: Pilgrimages of Pain and Hope and the Economics of Eating Together." In: *Mission Studies*, 29 (2012), 183–200.

Second, *ethics*. The text about love that we find in 1 Cor 13 is in the context of diversity and deep disagreements. Believers in that context, for example, differed as to what they could eat or not eat. These same believers make different decisions regard this ethical problem, decisions made possible because Scripture itself does not give a definitive answer. In this context, the apostle Paul urges love. From this example, it seems that diversity and even disagreements are required in the body of Christ if we want to know the meaning of unity, love, forgiveness, patience and self-denial. It is easy to love others who think the same as you think, but are we able to do so with those that think differently?

Third, *vision*. On the road to Emmaus, the disciples found out the truth about Jesus' resurrection only when they sat down and had dinner together – with Jesus at the centre – in spite of their differences. During the long walk from Jerusalem, they resisted the tendency of walking away from each other due to their divergent theological understandings of the Messiah. They did not find Jesus through the long hours of theological arguing. Their eyes were open only when they shared a meal. We gain a new vision of other followers of Christ – and about Christ himself – when we see people not as our opposites but as members of our family. With family, it is possible to sit and eat together in spite of our differences.

### 4. THE FULFILMENT OF OUR MISSION IS HOPE

The joyful expectation of God's coming offers vitality to our lives. The expectation of the fulfilment of God's promises to us is what allows us to pay full attention to the road on which we are walking. Paying attention to that road will allow us, in the words of German theologian Jürgen Moltmann, to "perceive things not just as they have become and now exist but also in the different ways they could be."[134] Our life needs to be eschatologically oriented.

We can look to the future that is revealed by God – a future without economic inequality, nationalisms, racism and exclusion – and, in this light, denounce, criticize and look for ways of changing current circumstances that contradict such a future. As Johannes Baptist Metz claims in their book *Faith in History and Society*, the imminent coming of a final point in history – a point in which justice and restoration will be a present reality – brings hope and strength in order to transform current realities of injustice, suffering, and oppression. In other words, we can look to the future that is revealed by God and based on it denounce, criticize and look for ways of changing present realities that contradict such a future. "Hope is here reclaimed as imminent expectation,"[135] writes Metz.

We can become free from the world around us and resist its pressures when we do not accept, according to Moltmann, "the so-called normative force of what is fact, because [we] know that a better world is possible and that changes in the present are necessary. Being able to wait means resisting the threats and seductions of the present, not letting oneself be brought into line, and not conforming."[136] It is in the process of not conforming that we find a new identity and fellowship. This new identity must be more important for us than the old one. "We are Christians first of all, and only after that are we members of our own particular country,"

---

[134] Jürgen Moltmann, *Ethics of Hope* (Minneapolis: Fortress Press, 2012), 3.
[135] Johannes Baptist Metz, *Faith in History and Society: Toward a Practical Fundamental Theology* trans. James Matthew Ashley, (New York: Crossroad Pub. Co., 2007), 82.
[136] Moltmann, 7.

concludes Moltmann.[137] This means we should develop a kingdom of God mentality instead of a nationalistic mentality.

Around one hundred years ago, a German Mennonite pastor and historian, Christian Neff, had a dream about inviting Anabaptist churches from around the world to connect to one another. In a context of suffering because of World War I and revolutions, he explained his vision in the following way: "Our strength is great if we stand united in one faith and remain loyal to the brotherhood."[138]

A unified, global fellowship gives us strength and hope in spite of suffering. Neff understood this as well as his brothers and sisters of Russia, who, in the midst of suffering and persecution at that time, supported his vision and encouraged him in his desire of building a global Mennonite communion. However, not every Mennonite leader in Europe agreed with Neff. Why to have another Mennonite institution? Do we need something like a global interdependency?

It is easy to get Neff's vision when you are dealing with contexts of suffering and oppression. Churches in contexts like this appreciate the support and hope they find in a global family of faith. On the other hand, churches that are in contexts of affluence and comfort tend to live independently, without seeing the value of a global community. There are wealthy churches who appear concerned about taking God's kingdom to other places yet fail to notice that an essential part of that kingdom means being a global, interdependent church that is able to walk alongside members who suffer and celebrate with those who experience joy.

---

[137] Ibid. 40.

[138] Cited by John Lapp and Ed van Straten in "Mennonite World Conference 1925–2000: From Euro-American Conference to Worldwide Communion," *The Mennonite Quarterly Review* (January 2003), 8–9.

As followers of Jesus, we are called to walk alongside those that suffer, to stand with them, and to try to stop the cycle of violence as Jesus did. In the words of the Mennonite theologian Norman Kraus:

> Jesus' *shalom-making* was a ministry of the "wounded healer" who healed through transformation. Instead of leading a violent revolution as the insurgents of his day advocated or working at political reform of the oppressing structures, he identified with the poor and attempted to interrupt the cycle of violence. At the same time he by no means condoned the inequities of the system fuelled by the selfish anxiety of the politically and economically powerful. This nonviolent peacebuilding from the bottom up is the essential message of Jesus.[139]

## CONCLUSION

Let's think as citizens of a new nation in which there is not a gap between rich and poor, but where economic equality exists between all people. Let's think as citizens of a new nation in which there is not racial discrimination, but where cultural diversity is affirmed and celebrated. Let's continue experiencing the reality of this new kingdom among us today. Let's continue sending micro-communities that live out this kind of mission. Our church is called to be a foretaste of the kingdom! That is our mission!

---

[139] C. Norman Kraus, *The Jesus Factor in Justice and Peacemaking*, Theological Postings Series (Telford, Pa.: Cascadia Pub. House, 2011), 114.

## STUDY QUESTIONS

1. Name an example of a mission that reflects the definition of mission presented in this chapter. What positive aspects stand out from this experience? What challenges does it represent?
2. Name an example of a mission that differs from the definition of mission presented in this chapter. What consequences did this experience bring? What challenges does it represent?
3. What concrete forms of multicultural mission could be given?
4. Hope in the midst of suffering is fundamental for many Christians. Do you know of any personal experience or of a community where the support of other people helped overcome the pain and generated hope to move forward?

# Authors

**Antonio González** is from Spain and has a doctorate in philosophy (Universidad Pontificia de Comillas, Madrid) and a doctorate in theology (Philosophish-Theologische Hochshchule Sankt-Georgen, Frankfurt). He is the director of Study and Publications of the Xavier Zubiri Foundation. Antonio is a pastor of a Brethren in Christ church in Spain.

**César García** (MA, theology, Fresno Pacific Biblical Seminary) was born in Bogotá, Colombia. He is a member of Iglesias Hermanos Menonitas de Colombia (the Colombian Mennonite Brethren Church) and has served there as church planter, pastor and chair of the national Colombian MB church. Since 2012, César has been serving as general secretary of Mennonite World Conference.

**David W. Shenk** was born in Tanzania where his parents, Clyde and Alta Shenk, served as missionaries among the Zanaki people. They were pioneer missionaries beginning churches where Christ was not known. David was deeply formed in that experience of participating with them. After their marriage, David with Grace served as pioneers among the Somali Muslim peoples of northeastern Africa. After some years in East Africa, David and his family served in North America church planting. He has been a global leader in missions and peacemaker. He is a preacher, teacher and writer. His special interest is in bearing witness to Christ in a world of religious pluralism.

**James R. Krabill** is from United States and served with Mennonite Board of Missions (MBM) over a period of twenty years as a Bible and church history teacher among African-initiated churches in Ivory Coast. Since 1995, he has worked as vice president for MBM's mission advocacy and communication division and, since 2002, as senior executive for global ministries at Mennonite Mission Network. He is the general editor of *Worship and Mission for the Global Church: An Ethnodoxology Handbook* (2013).

**Janie Blough** is from France and has been serving as a mission worker under the auspices of Mennonite Mission Network (formerly Mennonite Board of Mission) in France since 1975 and is an active member of the Châtenay-Malabry Mennonite Church. She is co-director of the Paris Mennonite Centre and teaches liturgy-related courses and conducts training workshops in French-speaking Mennonite educational institutions and congregations, as well as other Christian educational centres and venues. Her masters and DMin degrees in worship studies are from the Robert E. Webber Institute for Worship Studies.

**Mvwala C. Katshinga** is a Congolese missiologist, linguist and leadership trainer for Bible translation. The associate pastor of a local congregation in Kinshasa, Mvwala directs the department of mission of the Communauté des Églises de Frères Mennonites au Congo (CEFMC – Mennonite Brethren conference). He is also a professor and researcher at the National Teacher Training University and at the University Centre for Missiology in Kinshasa, Democratic Republic of Congo.

**Nzash Lumeya** was born in Democratic Republic of Congo and now lives in United States. He has a PhD in missiology (Fuller Theological Seminary) and he is president and professor at Fresno School of Mission, Fresno, California, USA, and visiting professor at the University Centre for Missiology, Kinshasa, Democratic Republic of Congo.

**Petrus Eko Handoyo** and his wife Yuliana with their two young sons have been serving with Mennonite Mission Network and PIPKA, the mission agency of the Muria Christian Church of Indonesia (GKMI Synod), in Mongolia (2001–2011) and in the Kingdom of Cambodia (2012–now). He and his family are sent out by GKMI Gloria Patri, a Mennonite church in Semarang, Central Java, Indonesia. He holds a BPhil in philosophy from Gadjah Mada State University, Yogyakarta, Indonesia. He then studied theology at Baptist Theological Seminary of Indonesia, Semarang and at Cipanas Theological College, Indonesia, and completed a Master Divinity program in theology at Cipanas Theological College. Now, he is a PhD student in the intercultural studies program at Bethany International University, Singapore. He previously taught at the Union Bible Theological College and Mongolia International University in Ulaanbaatar, Mongolia, and later at the department of theology, Life University and University of Management and Economics in Sihanoukville, Cambodia. His research interests include axiology (philosophy of value) and Mongolian nomadism. He had written three value-related books, including *Steppe Call: A Missional Journey into a Mongolian Nomadic Life* (Andi Publishing, 2016).

**Rafael Zaracho** is a professor at the *Instituto Biblico Asuncion*. He holds a BA in theology (Instituto Biblico Asuncion), a master in theology (Fresno, California, USA), and a PhD in theology (St. Andrews University, United Kingdom). He is the secretary of the Mission Commission of Mennonite World Conference. He is the director of a research centre called *Marturia* and the director of a theological journal called *Espacio Teológico*. Rafael and Rut have two young children, Sofía and Sebastian, and are members of the *Iglesia Cristiana de la Paz* (Mennonite Brethren) in Paraguay.

**Stanley W. Green** was born in South Africa and now lives in United States. He is the executive director of Mennonite Mission Network, the mission agency of Mennonite Church USA. He has served in mission agency leadership for the past twenty-five years. He is also currently chair of the Mission Commission of Mennonite World Conference. He has led congregations in South Africa, California and Jamaica where he and his spouse Ursula Lucille served as mission workers in the 1980s. Stanley has a postgraduate degree in intercultural studies from Fuller Theological Seminary in Pasadena, California. He has served on several boards, travelled and ministered in more than eighty countries around the world.

**Victor Pedroza Cruz** is from México. He is anthropologist and professor of history. He and his wife (Ofelia García) are missionaries and pastors in Chihuahua, México.